A GUIDE TO

TWELFTH NIGHT OR WHAT YOU WILL

RUTH COLEMAN

WITH TONY BUZAN

Hodder & Stoughton

Cover photograph ©: The Kobal Collection
Mind Maps: Philip Chambers
Illustrations: Karen Donnelly

ISBN 0 340 75348 X

First published 1999
Impression number 10 9 8 7 6 5 4 3 2 1
Year 2002 2001 2000 1999

Typeset by Transet Limited, Coventry, England.
Printed in Great Britain for Hodder & Stoughton Educational, a division of
Hodder Headline Plc, 338 Euston Road, London NW1 3BH by Cox and Wyman Ltd,
Reading, Berks.

Contents

There are five important things you must know about your brain and memory to revolutionize the way you study:

- how your memory ('recall') works *while* you are learning
- how your memory works *after* you have finished learning
- how to use Mind Maps – a special technique for helping you with all aspects of your studies
- how to increase your reading speed
- how to prepare for tests and exams.

Recall during learning

– THE NEED FOR BREAKS

When you are studying, your memory can concentrate, understand and remember well for between 20 and 45 minutes at a time. Then it needs a break. If you carry on for longer than this without a break your memory starts to break down. If you study for hours non-stop, you will remember only a small fraction of what you have been trying to learn, and you will have wasted hours of valuable time.

So, ideally, *study for less than an hour*, then take a five to ten minute break. During the break listen to music, go for a walk, do some exercise, or just daydream. (Daydreaming is a necessary brain-power booster – geniuses do it regularly.) During the break your brain will be sorting out what it has been learning, and you will go back to your books with the new information safely stored and organized in your memory banks. We recommend breaks at regular intervals as you work through the Literature Guides. Make sure you take them!

Recall *after learning*

– THE WAVES OF YOUR MEMORY

What do you think begins to happen to your memory straight after you have finished learning something? Does it immediately start forgetting? No! Your brain actually *increases* its power and carries on remembering. For a short time after your study session, your brain integrates the information, making a more complete picture of everything it has just learnt. Only then does the rapid decline in memory begin, and as much as 80 per cent of what you have learnt can be forgotten in a day.

However, if you catch the top of the wave of your memory, and briefly review (look back over) what you have been studying at the correct time, the memory is stamped in far more strongly, and stays at the crest of the wave for a much longer time. To maximize your brain's power to remember, take a few minutes and use a Mind Map to review what you have learnt at the end of a day. Then review it at the end of a week, again at the end of a month, and finally a week before your test or exam. That way you'll ride your memory wave all the way there – and beyond!

The *Mind Map* ®

– A PICTURE OF THE WAY YOU THINK

Do you like taking notes? More importantly, do you like having to go back over and learn them before tests or exams? Most students I know certainly do not! And how do you take your notes? Most people take notes on lined paper, using blue or black ink. The result, visually, is boring! And what does *your* brain do when it is bored? It turns off, tunes out, and goes to sleep! Add a dash of colour, rhythm, imagination, and the whole note-taking process becomes much more fun, uses more of your brain's abilities, and improves your recall and understanding.

A Mind Map mirrors the way your brain works. It can be used for note-taking from books or in class, for reviewing what you have just studied, and for essay planning for coursework and in tests or exams. It uses all your memory's natural techniques to build up your rapidly growing 'memory muscle'.

You will find Mind Maps throughout this book. Study them, add some colour, personalize them, and then have a go at drawing your own – you'll remember them far better! Stick them in your files and on your walls for a quick-and-easy review of the topic.

HOW TO DRAW A MIND MAP

1. Start in the middle of the page. This gives your brain the maximum room for its thoughts.
2. Always start by drawing a small picture or symbol. Why? Because a picture is worth a thousand words to your brain. And try to use at least three colours, as colour helps your memory even more.
3. Let your thoughts flow, and write or draw your ideas on coloured branching lines connected to your central image. These key symbols and words are the headings for your topic. Start like the Mind Map on page 8.
4. Then add facts and ideas by drawing more, smaller, branches on to the appropriate main branches, just like a tree.
5. Always print your word clearly on its line. Use only one word per line.
6. To link ideas and thoughts on different branches, use arrows, colours, underlining, and boxes (see page 18).

HOW TO READ A MIND MAP

1. Begin in the centre, the focus of your topic.
2. The words/images attached to the centre are like chapter headings; read them next.
3. Always read out from the centre, in every direction (even on the left-hand side, where you will have to read from right to left, instead of the usual left to right).

USING MIND MAPS

Mind Maps are a versatile tool – use them for taking notes in class or from books, for solving problems, for brainstorming with friends, and for reviewing and working for tests or exams – their uses are endless! You will find them invaluable for planning essays for coursework and exams. Number your main branches in the order in which you want to use them and off you go – the main headings for your essay are done and all your ideas are logically organized!

Super speed reading

It seems incredible, but it's been proved – the faster you read, the more you understand and remember! So here are some tips to help you to practise reading faster – you'll cover the ground more quickly, remember more, and have more time left for both work and play.

- First read the whole text (whether it's a lengthy book or an exam or test paper) very quickly, to give your brain an overall idea of what's ahead and get it working. (It's like sending out a scout to look at the territory you have to cover – it's much easier when you know what to expect!) Then read the text again for more detailed information.
- Have the text a reasonable distance away from your eyes. In this way your eye/brain system will be able to see more at a glance, and will naturally begin to read faster.
- Take in groups of words at a time. Rather than reading 'slowly and carefully' read faster, more enthusiastically.
- Take in phrases rather than single words while you read.
- Use a guide. Your eyes are designed to follow movement, so a thin pencil underneath the lines you are reading, moved smoothly along, will 'pull' your eyes to faster speeds.

Preparing for tests and exams

- Review your work systematically. Cram at the start of your course, not the end, and avoid 'exam panic'!
- Use Mind Maps throughout your course, and build a Master Mind Map for each subject – a giant Mind Map that summarizes everything you know about the subject.
- Use memory techniques such as mnemonics (verses or systems for remembering things like dates and events).
- Get together with one or two friends to study, compare Mind Maps, and discuss topics.

AND FINALLY...

Have *fun* while you learn – it has been shown that students who make their studies enjoyable understand and remember everything better and get the highest grades. I wish you and your brain every success!

(Tony Buzan)

HOW TO USE THIS GUIDE

This guide assumes that you have already read *Twelfth Night,* although you could read 'Background' and 'The story of *Twelfth Night'* before that. It is best to use this guide alongside the play. You could read 'Who's Who?' and 'Themes' without referring to the play, but you will get more out of these sections if you do refer to it to check the points made in these sections, and especially when tackling the questions designed to test your recall and help you to think about the play.

The sections

The 'Commentary' section can be used in a number of ways. One way is to read a scene or part of a scene in the play, and then read the commentary for that section. Keep on until you come to a test section, test yourself – then have a break! Alternatively, read the Commentary for a scene or part of a scene, then read that scene in the play, then go back to the Commentary. Find out what works best for you.

'Topics for discussion and brainstorming' gives topics that could well feature in exams or provide the basis for coursework. It would be particularly useful for you to discuss them with friends, or brainstorm them using Mind Map techniques (see p. vi).

'How to get an "A" in English Literature' gives valuable advice on what to look for in a text, and what skills you need to develop in order to achieve your personal best.
'The exam essay' is a useful 'night before' reminder of how to tackle exam questions, and 'Model answer' gives an example of an A-grade essay and the Mind Map and plan used to write it.

The questions

Whenever you come across a question in the guide with a star ✪ in front of it, think about it for a moment. You could even jot down a few words in rough to focus your mind. There is not usually a 'right' answer to these questions: it is important for you to develop your own opinions if you want to get an 'A'. The 'Test yourself' sections are designed to take you about

10–20 minutes each – which will be time well spent. Take a short break after each one.

L*ine numbers*

Line references are to the *New Penguin Shakespeare* edition. If you have another edition, the line numbers may be slightly different, although the Act and scene numbers will normally be the same.

K*ey to icons*

THEMES

A **theme** is an idea explored by an author. Whenever a theme is dealt with in the guide, the appropriate icon is used. This means you can find where a theme is mentioned just by flicking through the book. Go on – try it now!

Love 

Appearance and reality 

Chaos and order 

Melancholy 

This icon is used in the Commentary wherever there is a special section on the author's choice of words and imagery.

Background

Twelfth Night is a delightful romantic comedy incorporating many elements of farce. It looks at imaginary events taking place at the end of the Christmas period when people have let go of their everyday cares and have time to do, as the play is subtitled, *what you will*. In Elizabethan times, festivals held at this time of year turned the usual order upside down. There is evidence of a reversal of everyday order taking place in the Court of Misrule held at one of the Inns of Court in London each year about twelve days after Christmas when a Lord of Misrule took the place of the lawlords and churchmen who normally presided over the court.

This reversal of the usual order is reflected in the interests and behaviour of the characters in *Twelfth Night*. Viola, Orsino and Olivia are embroiled in a romantic triangle of unrequited love, misunderstanding is heaped upon misunderstanding, and those with a taste for the low life indulge themselves in revelry, mischief and playfulness. Malvolio, the Puritan, pays the price for his serious attitude to life and becomes a scapegoat for the revellers.

The play is a witty and lighthearted musical and the key musician is Feste the clown. His role, the songs he sings, and the antics of those who enjoy Olivia's hospitality, give the play something of the flavour of a pantomime, such as you might see in any theatre at Christmas. By the end of the play several different kinds of love have been presented and the revellers begin to pay for their fun. Life in Illyria is returning to normal, except for Malvolio, whose humiliation makes him thirst bitterly for revenge.

Source material

The play was written in about 1600 and there are several theories about its sources. There were certainly plays and stories being performed in Europe which may have given Shakespeare some of the inspiration for the ideas he explores in *Twelfth Night*.

POLITICS & COMMERCE

THE AGE OF

1580 - FRANCIS DRAKE BECAME FIRST ENGLISHMAN TO CIRCUMNAVIGATE THE WORLD

1586 - SIR WALTER RALEIGH IMPORTS TOBACCO FROM VIRGINIA USA

POTATO BROUGHT FROM COLOMBIA S.AMERICA

1587 - MARY QUEEN OF SCOTS (COUSIN TO ELIZABETH) EXECUTED AFTER FAILING TO RESTORE CATHOLICISM

QUEEN ELIZABETH I (1533-1603)

1588 - SPANISH ARMADA DEFEATED (129 SHIPS). ENGLAND DOMINATES THE SEAS

1605 - GUY FAWKES' GUNPOWDER PLOT TO BLOW UP HOUSES OF PARLIAMENT

1620 PILGRIM FATHERS BECOME FIRST ENGLISH SETTLERS IN NEW WORLD OF AMERICA

THIS PERIOD IS ALSO KNOWN AS THE LATE RENAISSANCE, THE TERM USED TO DESCRIBE GREAT ADVANCEMENT OF KNOWLEDGE IN SCIENCE, ART, NAVIGATION AND COMMERCE.

SHAKESPEARE

$a+b^2$

1579 – DEVELOPMENTS IN ALGEBRA & OTHER BRANCHES OF MATHS

FIRST GLASS EYES MADE

1582 – GREGORIAN CALENDER REPLACED WITH JULIAN IN EUROPE – USED EVER SINCE

1593 – PLAYWRIGHT CHRISTOPHER MARLOWE KILLED IN TAVERN BRAWL

WILLIAM SHAKESPEARE (1564–1616)

1594 – TINTORETTO's DEATH FOLLOWS THAT OF OTHER GREAT ARTISTS LEONARDO, MICHELANGELO & RAPHAEL

GALILEO (1564–1642) MAKES GREAT ADVANCES IN PHYSICS, MATHS & ASTRONOMY IDEAS UNPOPULAR WITH CHURCH

1597 – IMPORTANT CHEMISTRY TEXT BOOK PUBLISHED (LIBAVIUS)

FIRST TELESCOPE (LIPPERSHEY)

1599 – FIRST SERIOUS WORK IN ZOOLOGY PUBLISHED (ALDROVANDI)

IT ENDED THE MIDDLE AGES AND BEGAN MODERN TIMES

He probably also drew on his some of his own earlier plays such as *The Comedy of Errors* and *As You Like It* for material. We can also be fairly certain that some of the songs in the play are adaptations of what can be considered Elizabethan pop music. These elements are woven together with the craft of a mature and experienced playwright who knew how to 'work' his audience.

There are several theories regarding who the play was written for, and where and when it was first performed. It has long been considered certain that Queen Elizabeth commissioned it to be performed in January 1601 to honour a visiting Italian Duke named Orsino. However, there are equally convincing counter arguments to suggest that the first performance would not have taken place to coincide with the real Orsino's visit to court mainly because the Duke could have been offended by the play and its flouting of court etiquette.

Whether or not there was an earlier performance of the play, there is documentary evidence that *Twelfth Night* was definitely performed at the Middle Temple, one of the Inns of Court, in 1602 to celebrate the annual festival of misrule. The jokes and references to the legalities surrounding Sir Andrew's challenge to Viola/Cesario to enter into a duel support the theory that the play was written to be performed in the company of the legal students and professionals who learned and practised there.

Whoever the play was written for, Shakespeare's audiences would have lapped up the antics, jokes and misunderstandings that drive the action. They would leave the theatre feeling that they had enjoyed top quality entertainment and had a thoroughly good time, as we do today.

The comic aspects of *Twelfth Night* are perhaps easier to understand than those in some of Shakespeare's other plays because they share many of the same elements of the comedy we enjoy today. We witness clowning, knockabout exchanges, mistaken identities leading to confusion and the use of wit in language. The skill with which these humourous episodes are written has ensured that the play has endured the test of time to remain a festive favourite in many modern theatre and television productions.

The Story of *Twelfth Night*

The ruler of Illyria, Count Orsino, wallows in unrequited love for the countess Olivia. Viola is rescued from a shipwreck in another part of the kingdom. Viola is heartbroken because she believes that her twin brother Sebastian has drowned in the same shipwreck. Viola learns of Orsino and Olivia, and decides to become Orsino's servant disguised as a youth called Cesario. Viola, dressed as Cesario, is sent to woo Olivia on Orsino's behalf, but Olivia falls in love with Viola/Cesario, who has fallen in love with Orsino. It is revealed that Sebastian has been saved from the shipwreck by the loyal Antonio who decides to go with his friend to Illyria – even though he may be arrested by Orsino's men for a crime he has committed in the past.

Sir Toby Belch is Olivia's uncle. He invites his foolish friend, Sir Andrew Aguecheek, to try to win Olivia. Both of them flirt with Maria, Olivia's maid, and Feste the clown joins them in drunken revelry at Olivia's house. Malvolio, a senior servant to Olivia tells them off and so Maria designs a prank to teach him a lesson for being such a killjoy. The pranksters hide in a tree to watch Malvolio's reaction to finding some love letters apparently written to him by Olivia. Although they have actually been written by Maria, Malvolio falls into the trap and flatters himself that Olivia is in love with him. The letters instruct him to smile and wear ridiculous yellow stockings with cross-garters.

Having made an excuse to make Viola/Cesario return to her, Olivia confesses her love and is turned down. Maria, Sir Toby and Olivia's servant Fabian, decide to play another prank by getting Sir Andrew to challenge Viola/Cesario to a duel to impress Olivia. The pranksters make sure that the cowardly Sir Andrew and Viola/Cesario are terrified of each other. Malvolio makes such a fool of himself that Olivia thinks he is going mad and discharges him into the care of Sir Toby who locks him in a dark cell.

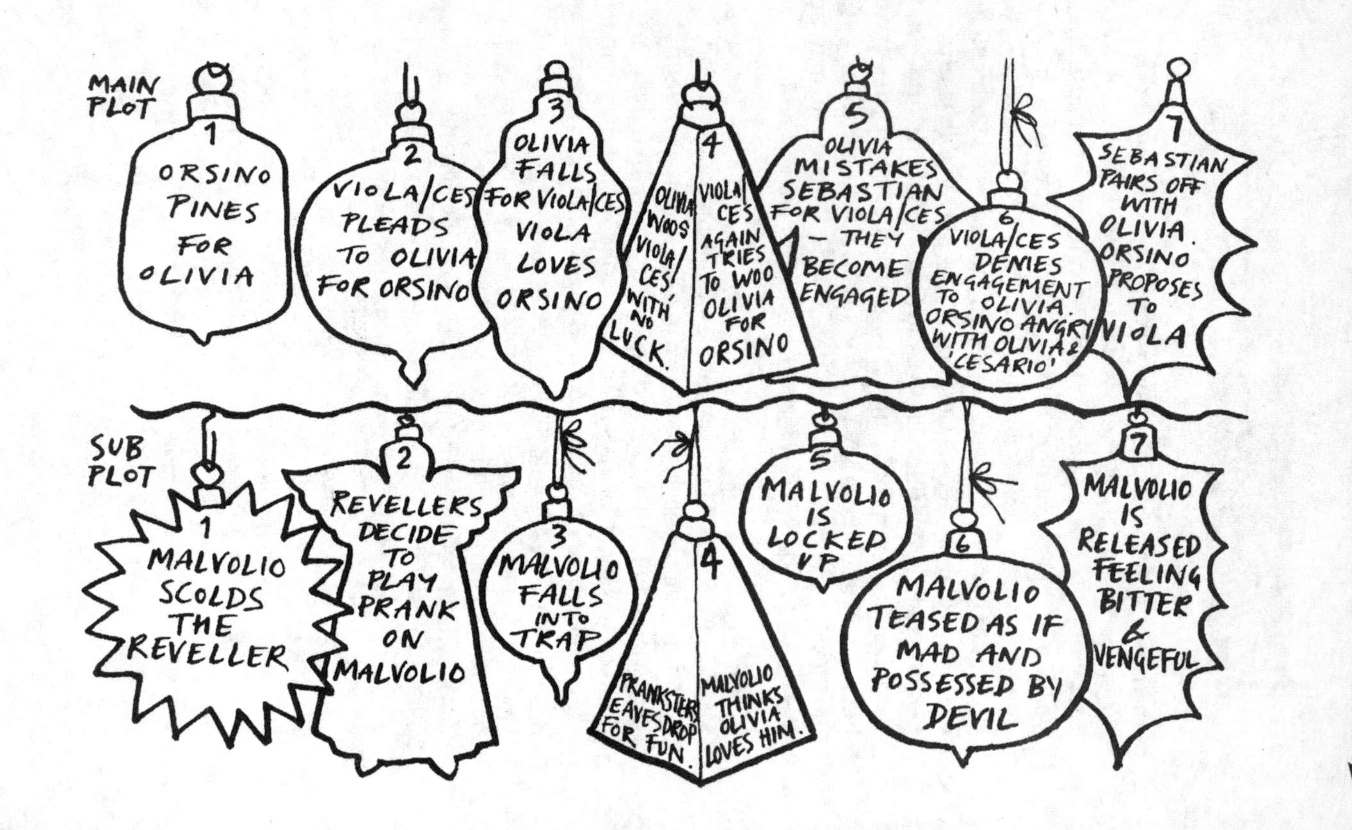

MAIN PLOT
1 ORSINO PINES FOR OLIVIA
2 VIOLA/CES PLEADS TO OLIVIA FOR ORSINO
3 OLIVIA FALLS FOR VIOLA/CES VIOLA LOVES ORSINO
4 OLIVIA WOOS VIOLA/CES' WITH NO LUCK.
VIOLA/CES AGAIN TRIES TO WOO OLIVIA FOR ORSINO
5 OLIVIA MISTAKES SEBASTIAN FOR VIOLA/CES – THEY BECOME ENGAGED
6 VIOLA/CES DENIES ENGAGEMENT TO OLIVIA. ORSINO ANGRY WITH OLIVIA & 'CESARIO'
7 SEBASTIAN PAIRS OFF WITH OLIVIA. ORSINO PROPOSES TO VIOLA
SUB PLOT
1 MALVOLIO SCOLDS THE REVELLER
2 REVELLERS DECIDE TO PLAY PRANK ON MALVOLIO
3 MALVOLIO FALLS INTO TRAP
4 PRANKSTERS EAVESDROP FOR FUN.
MALVOLIO THINKS OLIVIA LOVES HIM.
5 MALVOLIO IS LOCKED UP
6 MALVOLIO TEASED AS IF MAD AND POSSESSED BY DEVIL
7 MALVOLIO IS RELEASED FEELING BITTER & VENGEFUL

As the duel is about to take place, Antonio arrives to save Viola/Cesario, whom he believes to be Sebastian. Antonio is arrested by Orsino's men and thinks he is being betrayed by Sebastian because Viola/Cesario does not recognize him. Soon the pranksters encounter Sebastian, who, unlike Viola/Cesario for whom they mistake him, shocks them by his readiness to fight. Olivia also meets Sebastian and mistakes him for his twin. Sebastian finds her familiarity with him strange, but is delighted that she loves him.

Egged on by the pranksters, Feste dresses as a priest to further taunt Malvolio with talk of being possessed by the devil. Eventually, Feste agrees to take a letter from Malvolio to Olivia. Meanwhile, Olivia and Sebastian become formally engaged.

Viola/Cesario, still being mistaken for Sebastian, is accused of ingratitude by Antonio, and denies both being engaged to Olivia, and fighting Sir Andrew. Orsino is furious with both Olivia and Viola/Cesario. At last, the twins are reunited as Sebastian arrives on the scene to apologize for the fight, declare his love for Olivia, and delight at seeing Antonio again. Orsino shifts his affection from Olivia to Viola, whom he decides to marry. As the two pairs of lovers prepare to celebrate their good fortune, Olivia reads Malvolio's letters, sends for him and the prank is explained. In his humiliation, Malvolio swears revenge. Feste closes the play with a song.

Over to you

- ? Now you've read the background, study this key point summary and start your own Mind Map of the play.
- ? Picture some of the scenes and costumes from this drama and create your own mental video or draw some sketches of them.

now you know what's what, take a break before getting to know who's who

This Mini Mind Map summarizes the character groups in *Twelfth Night*. Add to it yourself as you work your way through this section, and then compare it with the full Mind Map on p. 18.

Orsino, Duke of Illyria

The ruler of the imaginary land Illyria is an eligible young nobleman. He is reputed to be a fair man who is able to command great loyalty from his courtiers. As the captain says of him to Viola: *A noble Duke, in nature as in name.*

ORSINO THE LOVER

Orsino is the first character we meet in *Twelfth Night*. He wallows in a self-indulgent melancholy mood listening to music as he indulges his passion for Olivia. He seems rather underemployed since he has the time to think about her, instead of affairs of state. Orsino is accustomed to having what he wants, and cannot accept Olivia's rebuttal, despite Viola/Cesario's efforts to make him see that his goddess is not interested in him. With the vanity and self-assuredness that comes with his social status, Orsino simply cannot believe that Olivia can seriously mean to turn him down.

This certainty that he can have whatever he wants is revealed again later when he becomes engaged to Viola. He is, of course, secure in the knowledge that Viola loves him, but his way of proposing to her is shaped in the form of a command rather than a request. In matters of the heart he is convinced that he knows best. He also has very clear views about what makes a successful romantic partnership – the woman should be younger than the man, women cannot love as deeply as men, and men value physical attractiveness more highly than women. ✪ How far do you agree with him?

A NASTY TEMPER

There are two other things to note about Orsino. He is apparently in love with Olivia, but very quickly transfers his affection to Viola when Olivia is finally lost to him and Viola's true sex is revealed. ✪ What do you think this says about him? He also shows a vengeful side and a nasty temper when he does not get his own way. Look at the way he threatens to kill Olivia and then Viola/Cesario. ✪ Do you think he means it or is he just venting his anger?

Viola/Cesario

Twin to Sebastian, we never know where Viola and her brother were going when they were shipwrecked or why she chooses to disguise herself. We must assume that she wants to conceal her identity until she has gathered more information about where she is and will feel safer dressed as a boy. Perhaps she simply wants to collect her thoughts and privately mourn the brother she thinks she has lost. Shakespeare of course, had another reason for her disguise – the plot is largely driven by making 'Cesario' the focus of most of the misunderstandings that take place. Viola is the innocent device around which much of the comedy revolves.

A CONSTANT FORCE

Viola is a likeable, well-rounded character, described by her brother as *accounted beautiful* with *a mind that envy could not but call fair.* As Cesario, she quickly becomes Orsino's chosen confidante and messenger, later to be loved by him as Viola. Her eloquence and the integrity with which she conducts herself ensures that she is also the object of Olivia's affections. She generously offers Antonio half of her purse when he saves her from the duel, even though she does not know him.

Viola is also selfless and accepting of fate and the limitations it places upon her. She never wavers from sincerely representing Orsino to Olivia, despite her own love for the count. When she realizes that Olivia has fallen in love with her and that she has become caught up in a love triangle, she knows there is little she can do, saying: *O time, thou must untangle this, not I!/ It is too hard a knot for me t'untie.* Until her twin displays the same quality, Viola is the only character to be constant and unshakeable in the object of her love.

INNOCENT VICTIM

Viola gains our sympathy because she has a far harder time than any of the other nobles, partly because her disguise as Cesario frequently puts her in a difficult position. Not only does she have to represent Orsino to Olivia, but she becomes the innocent victim of Sir Toby's prank to set her up in a duel with Sir Andrew. Until Sebastian arrives to make sense of the misunderstanding, she is in the bad books of Orsino, Olivia, and Antonio, as well as the pranksters. She is dismissed by Sir Toby as *A very dishonest, paltry boy, and more a coward than a hare.*
✪ How much sympathy do you feel for Viola?

Sebastian

Twin to Viola, Sebastian has high status as a noble character, but appears on stage very little until the final act. He is mainly used by Shakespeare as a foil to Viola to create misunderstandings in the plot.

THE TWIN

Provident in peril, Sebastian shares many of his sister's qualities in addition to their physical similarity. He is deeply upset when he thinks his sister has drowned and is glad of the support Antonio offers him in his grief without wanting to be a bore about it. He is loyal to Antonio, does not pick fights, although he is brave and ready to defend himself when the pranksters challenge him.

THE LOVER

Like Orsino, Sebastian is quick to respond to a beautiful woman. He develops an affection for Olivia without reservation although he knows something is odd in the way she rushes to claim him. It is to his credit that he thanks good luck for her favour rather than flattering himself that he is 'God's gift to women' as Orsino might. He is indeed a fortunate young man – he suffers for the apparent loss of a sister but by the end of the play collects all the prizes without needing to make much effort. His character is largely defined by the way it mirrors that of his sister whom we get to know well and have a great deal of respect for. Sebastian is therefore presented as worthy of Olivia's love, and we are sure he will keep his word to her.

Two men

? In view of Orsino's comment:
Our fancies are more giddy and unfirm,
More longing, wavering, sooner lost and worn,
Than women's are. (Act 2, scene 4, lines 33-5)
what kind of husband do you think he will be to Viola?

? 'Sebastian exists more as a device to drive the plot than as a character'. How far do you agree?

? Using different coloured pens to represent Orsino and Sebastian, circle the words that apply to one, other, or both of them :
stubborn responsive sexist aggressive modest brave melancholy fickle infatuated musical authoritative impulsive grieving loyal
Add any other words which spring to mind as you think about these characters.

now take a break before meeting the lady of the house

Olivia the countess

Olivia shares the noble status of Orsino and the twins. She shows herself to be vain when she removes her veil in front of Viola, but not without good reason – she seems to be considered very beautiful by those who court her.

THE HEAD OF THE HOUSE

As the head of the household, Olivia seems to be quite relaxed about what goes on there despite the scoldings that Maria and Malvolio give to the revellers who are her house guests. Sir Toby, her uncle, seems to live there and 'live it up'; she does not apparently object to Sir Andrew being invited to stay, and she only really pretends to mind when Feste, the clown has gone absent without leave. Her tolerance of, and respect for, her servants shows in several ways. Feste knows he can get away with his absence, and it never occurs to Maria, the maid, that Olivia could be very angry with her for forging her handwriting in the letters left for Malvolio.

Olivia's fairness is again revealed when she tries to find out who has so *notoriously abused* Malvolio, and later, accepting Fabian's explanation that he deserved it. She treats her servants with respect and does not pull rank over them, but is capable of organizing her own affairs efficiently. We hear that she can:

> *... sway her house, command her followers,*
> *Take and give back affairs and their dispatch,*
> *With such a smooth, discreet, and stable bearing*
> (Act 4, scene 3, lines 17–19)

✪ Who says this about her and why?

OLIVIA IN LOVE

In contrast to Viola who has also lost a brother, she is showy in the way she grieves her dead brother and swears to wear mourning clothes for years. She is, however, quick to snap out of her melancholy mood when she meets Viola/Cesario and reveals herself to be very determined and forward. In this respect she resembles Orsino – she is wallowing in melancholy when we first meet her, she will not take 'no' for an answer from the object of her affections and she knows what she wants and is used to getting it.

Olivia is also sharp and quick-witted. This is evidenced in the speed with which she thinks of sending Malvolio off with the ring as an excuse to bring Viola/Cesario back. She later marches Sebastian off to the church before he can change his mind.

Two women

? Does Viola get what she deserves?

? Name the three suitors to Olivia.

? Mind Map the things that Viola and Olivia have in common. It may help you think about status, grief, and love.

take a break from the lovers before some clowning around ...

Malvolio

Olivia's senior servant, Malvolio is the most complex character in the play. As steward or manager, he is employed to keep order and maintain the household, which he seems to do with humourless efficiency. We see little of him doing his job, except for the episode (Act 2, scene 3) when he perhaps not unreasonably chastises the drunken revellers for their noisy fun. So much do they resent his killjoy nature, however, that this proves to be the last straw and they hatch their plot against him. We only really witness this example of his management style. ✪ Do you think it mean-spirited of Malvolio to say he will report the revels to Olivia?

THE PRANK

Malvolio has the kind of self-absorbed character that fails to pick up the signals that make for successful social interaction and ensure popularity. It is this lack of social skills that Maria exploits in dreaming up exactly the sort of prank that Malvolio will fall for. He would almost certainly be respectful of his mistress, and there is evidence of him being over obliging in her presence (Act 1, scene 5). It is rather sad and pathetic that he falls for the prank so easily, but it shows that he is just as human as anyone else and has the same desires. The way Shakespeare presents him, however, makes the idea of him as Olivia's lover somehow disgusting although Olivia certainly values and respects him. Her comment on his odd behaviour: *I would not have him miscarry for the half of my dowry* demonstrates this very clearly. He would like to marry Olivia, however, because such a marriage would raise his status considerably. Malvolio wants to believe Olivia loves him so he falls for the prank.

NOTORIOUSLY ABUSED

Whether Malvolio deserves the *notorious abuse* he is subjected to is for you to decide. One point to consider is that the play is about the festive season of Christmas when most people relax and do things they might not normally do. Someone as sober and dull as Malvolio would be an obvious target for mischief. Balancing this, however, is the fact that Malvolio is employed to run the house and keep order. Either way we are asked to accept Fabian's explanation to Olivia that he deserves the humiliation as a tit-for-tat: *If that the injuries be justly weighed/That have on both sides passed.* ✪ How easy do you think it would be for Malvolio to look Olivia in the eye again?

For more about Malvolio, see 'The exam essay', p. 79.

Feste the Clown

At our first viewing of Feste (Act 1, scene 5), we are made aware that we are meeting a free spirit who lives within his own rules rather than that of his mistress, Olivia. He soon impresses us with his eloquence, wit, and generally clever way with words and concepts such as his claim to be able to prove that someone is a fool.

MODERN PARALLELS

Feste is more likeable than Malvolio and Sir Andrew who prove to be the real fools. If Feste were a modern-day comic, he might be seen on TV or in cabaret. In the play he is part of a serving household, with Olivia, as patron, paying him to provide entertainment. In the days before media entertainment, wealthy people would pay entertainers to amuse them. Olivia uses him as she might a TV sit-com today, although he is also in the play to demonstrate the paradox that wisdom can co-exist with madness. Another difference is that, unlike a television set, Feste can answer back!

How widespread the use of fools was in Elizabethan England is hard to say, but Shakespeare used them in more than one play. In his famous tragedy, *King Lear,* a fool shows Lear how foolish he has been to reject a loving daughter. The fool was able to point out home truths in a way that no one else would be allowed to do.

As a multi-skilled entertainer, Feste delivers most of the music in the play. Although lowly in terms of rank, he also stands a little apart from the other servants. He is not involved in the prank to set up a duel between Viola and Sir Andrew and he only gets involved in tricking Malvolio when the steward taunts him – when Feste is disguised as 'Sir Topas'. Even then, he delivers to Malvolio the means to write the letter about his plight to Olivia although it is mischievous of him not to deliver it promptly.

Antonio

Along with the other sea captain who rescued Viola, Antonio is a sincere, loyal, brave and selfless friend to Sebastian. Both sea captains seem to have the role of guardian angel and protector to the hero twins in their adversity. This may be to reflect the chivalrous code of conduct expected of renaissance seafarers and explorers. Antonio has the additional role of being used to create more of the misunderstanding in which Viola becomes embroiled because of her resemblance to her absent brother. ✪ What do you think about the extreme degree of love that Antonio feels for Sebastian?

The pranksters

Sir Toby Belch, Sir Andrew Aguecheek and Maria are the comedians who live the low life and like a good time. Sir Toby is scheming, clever and happy to exploit a dullard for his own fun and to pay for his pleasure. He has a silvery tongue and is a real mischief-maker. His general attitude is summed up in the comment: *I am sure care's an enemy to life.* (Act 1, scene 3, line 2). ✪ What do you think he means by this?

Sir Andrew is sidekick to Sir Toby, and a very silly man. He pays for his and Sir Toby's revels, allows himself to be persuaded that Olivia could favour him and is set up for a duel in which he gives his horse to Sir Toby and receives a minor head wound. Sir Andrew is the fall-guy to Sir Toby's cleverness. Many of the jokes in the play arise from his inadequate grasp of words.

Olivia's maid, Maria, is a giggly, gossipping, good-time girl who may well be jealous of Malvolio. She takes liberties by imitating Olivia's writing and 'borrowing' her wax seal for letters, and knows she will get away with it. Being mischievously clever, she is a good match for Sir Toby, and she does not hesitate to tell him off for coming home late. ✪ What kind of marriage do you think they will have?

Fabian is really a minor player. He is needed to fan the flames of the prank to set up the duel, teasing Viola with false tales of Sir Andrew's fearsome courage, while Sir Toby does the same with Sir Andrew. In the final act it is quite big of him to take joint responsibility with Sir Toby for the plot against Malvolio and not to reveal to Olivia that Maria masterminded it.

Now try this

? Sort out these words into two lists to describe the characters of Malvolio and Sir Toby, adding others if you wish. The same words can appear in both lists:

puritan, prankster, drunk, sober, vain, self-loving, carefree, cunning, conniving, flirtatious, foolish, ridiculous, rowdy, comic, bawdy, efficient

Malvolio	Sir Toby

? Which of the characters do you like most? Why?

? Which of the characters do you like least? Why?

now you know about the people, take a break before you explore ideas

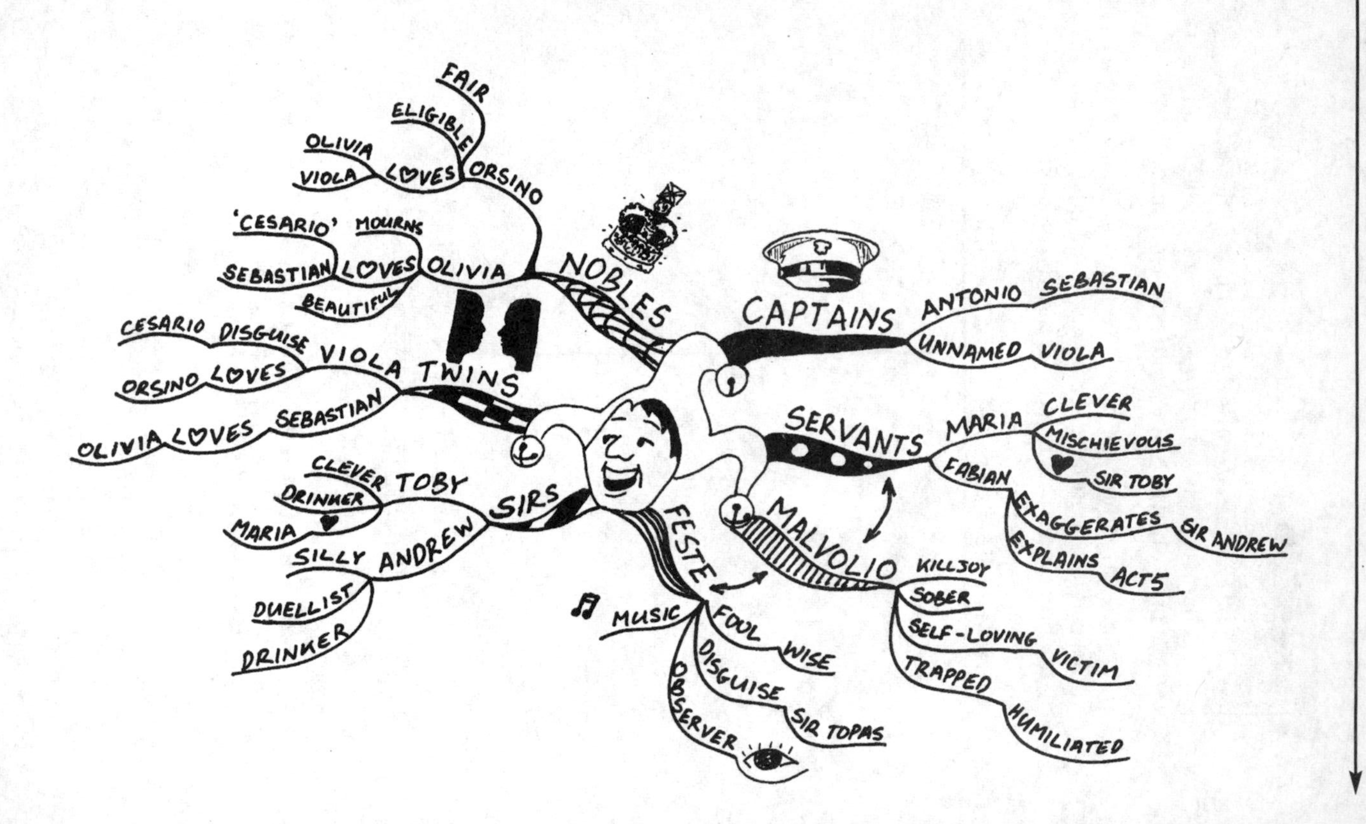
FAIR
ELIGIBLE
OLIVIA
VIOLA
LOVES
ORSINO
'CESARIO'
MOURNS
SEBASTIAN
LOVES
OLIVIA
BEAUTIFUL
NOBLES
CESARIO
DISGUISE
VIOLA
ORSINO
LOVES
TWINS
OLIVIA
LOVES
SEBASTIAN
CLEVER
TOBY
DRINKER
MARIA
SIRS
SILLY
ANDREW
DUELLIST
DRINKER
CAPTAINS
ANTONIO
SEBASTIAN
UNNAMED
VIOLA
SERVANTS
MARIA
CLEVER
MISCHIEVOUS
SIR TOBY
FABIAN
EXAGGERATES
SIR ANDREW
EXPLAINS
ACT5
MALVOLIO
KILLJOY
SOBER
SELF-LOVING
VICTIM
TRAPPED
HUMILIATED
FESTE
MUSIC
FOOL
WISE
DISGUISE
SIR TOPAS
OBSERVER

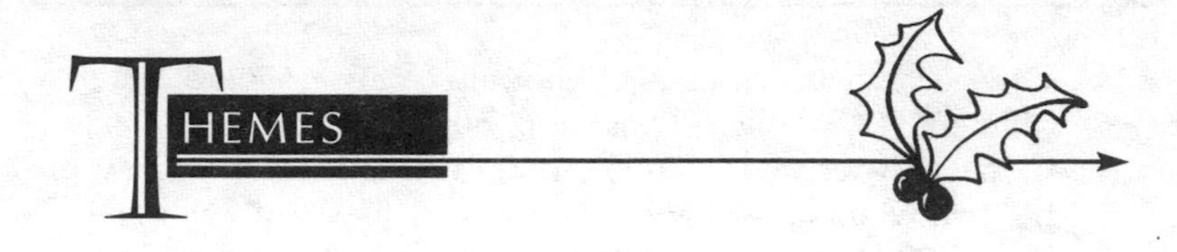

A theme is an idea developed or explored throughout a work (i.e. a play, book, poem, etc). The main themes of *Twelfth Night* are shown in the Mini Mind Map above. Test yourself on the themes by copying this Mind Map, adding to it yourself, and then comparing your results with the full Mind Map on p. 26.

Love

Shakespeare presents many facets of this main theme in his romantic comedy. We are presented with love between lovers, siblings, friends, servants and masters and the love of the good life. There are more sexual jokes and innuendos in *Twelfth Night* than in most of Shakespeare's other plays. Sexual matters are openly discussed between the lower orders, and they exist as a strong undercurrent between the nobles.

LOVE BETWEEN SIBLINGS

We hear most about Viola's grief for the brother she thinks she has lost at sea. This loss seems to be the main reason for her desire to hide her true identity. The grief of her brother, Sebastian, exactly mirrors Viola's because each believes the other to have perished in the shipwreck. The audience can enjoy knowing that at some point there will be a joyful reunion.

Olivia's love for her dead brother also mirrors Viola's, but in a different way. Viola still has some hope that her brother may be alive, whereas Olivia does not. The main contrast between the two women, however, is in the way they deal with their grief – Viola keeps it entirely to herself except for the captain who has saved her; Olivia's is a very public affair since she wears a veil, mourning dress and swears to remain in such clothes for seven years.

LOVE BETWEEN LOVERS

It is probably more correct to say that two kinds of love between lovers are presented in the play – imagined, and true, romantic love. In both cases, love at first sight is also a condition by which all the lovers are stricken. When Orsino first saw Olivia he thought *she purged the air of pestilence*; Viola is thoroughly in love with Orsino before three days have passed, Olivia complains that *Even so quickly may one catch the plague*; and Sebastian instantly falls in love with Olivia.

The play opens with Orsino indulging himself in his infatuation with Olivia. We do not know what has taken place between these two before the play opens, but we are quickly made aware that Olivia does not return Orsino's affection. Rather, his desire for her seems to be based upon worship from afar, instead of any kind of interaction between the two. Just look at the way Orsino not only sends someone else to do his wooing, but does not even write his own love speeches. Perhaps Orsino, who will not accept Olivia's rejection of him, simply wants a wife; the readiness with which he switches his attention to Viola would seem to bear this out.

To some degree the same may be said of Olivia. She falls in love with 'Cesario' without knowing 'he' is really a woman. The difference is that Shakespeare asks us to accept the idea that his twins are the same in thought and deed as they are alike physically.

THE LOVE TRIANGLE

Viola demonstrates true love most fully. From Act 1, scene 2 we are aware that she is on the lookout for a husband and wonders if Orsino might suit her. She quickly falls in love with him, but suffers the pain of knowing that he loves Olivia and that Olivia loves her in a triangle of unrequited love. Only Viola remains constantly and truly in love. Ultimately she is rewarded for her selfless patience when Orsino transfers his affection to her in a relationship based on mutual interaction rather than worship from a distance. The true love between them is echoed in the true and uncomplicated love that develops between Olivia and Sebastian. The marriage of Sir Toby to Maria also seems appropriate and mirrors the love of the two noble couples.

LOVE BETWEEN SERVANT AND MASTER

Whether or not Malvolio truly loves his mistress Olivia is debatable. It does not seem to have occurred to him to desire her until he thinks she is interested in him. Perhaps he has suppressed his feelings because their social status is unequal. ✪ What do you think?

The love between Orsino and his new servant Viola in the guise of Cesario is more genuine, and their betrothal at the end of the play seems appropriate.

LOVE BETWEEN FRIENDS

This aspect of love is demonstrated by the relationship between Sebastian and Antonio who saves him from the shipwreck. So great is Antonio's protective love for his friend that he risks his life by returning to Illyria where he is a wanted man. Antonio also unreservedly lends Sebastian his purse and draws dangerous attention to himself to save Viola/Cesario, (who he has mistaken for Sebastian), from the duel. Small wonder that he feels betrayed when Viola/Cesario does not recognize him.

LOVE OF THE GOOD LIFE

In contrast to the sober Malvolio, Sir Toby, Sir Andrew, Maria, Feste and Fabian like to have a good time. This involves drinking, jesting and generally making merry – usually at someone else's expense.

Appearance and reality

The most obvious way in which this theme is demonstrated is in Viola's disguise as the boy, Cesario. Her disguise misleads Orsino into thinking he has a loyal servant, makes Olivia fall into an impossible love, and ensures that Viola is mistaken for her twin which makes her vulnerable to fights and appearing disloyal. When Sebastian arrives in Illyria, Olivia believes him to be the 'Cesario' she has fallen in love with – again a mistake, but one which leads to a happy conclusion.

The deception that so humiliates Malvolio is a further key way in which Shakepeare presents the theme of appearance and reality. The humourless steward is set up to believe that Olivia loves him, when someone younger and more dashing would obviously suit her better. With the benefit of Malvolio's confinement, Feste is able to appear to be a priest rather than himself, echoing Viola's disguise.

Another manipulation of reality occurs when Sir Toby and Fabian manage to persuade Sir Andrew and Viola/Cesario that they have good cause to be terrified of each other.

Now try this

? Add the names of the lovers to each point of this triangle. Then draw arrows along the sides to show who loves who.

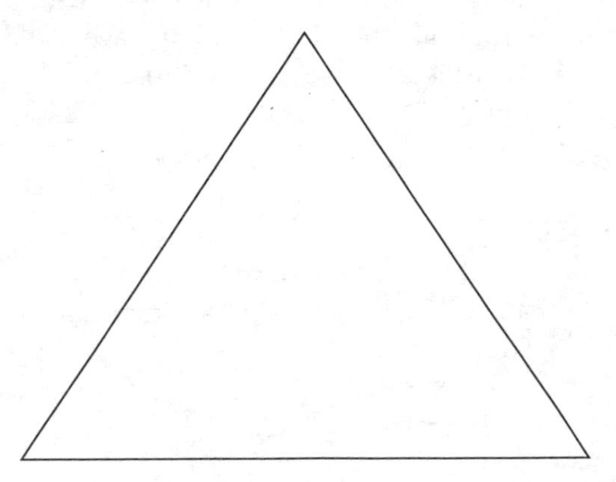

- ? Add your own view of the presentation of love to the Mini Mind Map at the start of this section.
- ? Find Feste's comment near the beginning of Act 4, scene 1 that could be taken to illustrate the theme of appearance and reality.

take a break from romance and reality before the chaos begins

Chaos and order

The development of this theme revolves around Viola's disguise as Cesario. The disguise sows the seeds for the chaos and disorder that reaches a peak at the start of Act 5. Although a certain amount of chaos is present in Olivia's household as a result of Sir Toby's revels, we are first presented with the chaos Viola is causing in Act 1, scene 5 when her disguise causes her to become the object of Olivia's desires. In Act 3, scene 4, Antonio draws attention to himself by protecting Viola/Cesario whom he has mistaken for Sebastian, and is arrested.

Thereafter, the play descends into chaos because Sebastian has made his way to Illyria but has not yet been introduced by name to those who live there. Fooled by the existence of two people who look the same, Antonio is the first to complain of the *ingrateful boy*. Soon Olivia appears to be perplexed by Viola/Cesario's denial of their marriage vows, which quickly turns Orsino's love for his beloved servant to anger. This muddle is added to when Sir Andrew enters the scene accusing Viola/Cesario of inflicting the head wound he has received from Sebastian and tells tales of Sir Toby suffering the same fate.

Revealing Sebastian's true identity brings an end to Viola's need for disguise. The revelation that there are two people so similar in appearance – but not in gender – clears up all the misunderstandings and unravels the muddles that have taken place before.

Feste as clown also plays a part in developing the theme of disorder. It is present in the many conceptual contradictions and the word-play in which he indulges. His transformation from clown to priest during his visit to Malvolio is also a reversal of the usual order. The play ends with Malvolio's release, his ordeal having been the result of a lack of order in Olivia's household. As the keeper of order he has been triumphed over by the forces of disorder. Now that the festive season, characterized by things being turned upside down, has ended, everything returns to normal.

Melancholy

This theme feeds off the theme of lost and unrequited love. It is present in the mood of the lovesick Orsino in the very first scene as he pines for the woman who will not return his affection. He calls for a serious song again in Act 2, scene 4 and after singing it, Feste says in parting: *Now the melancholy god protect thee.*

Olivia suffers from melancholy feelings because she has lost her brother. Maria fully exploits this mood to make the *sad and civil* Malvolio appear smiling in the cross-gartered yellow stockings that will: *be so unsuitable to her disposition – being addicted to a melancholy as she is.* By the time Malvolio actually does appear before Olivia she is suffering from the same kind of melancholy that Orsino is suffering – that her love for Viola/Cesario is not returned. On seeing the spectacle of Malvolio she comments that she sent for him *upon a sad occasion.*

Viola keeps her melancholy feelings hidden from the other characters but shares them with the audience. She does this in Act 2, scene 4 when she tells Orsino her own story as if it was someone else's to illustrate the strength of her love for him:

... She pined in thought,
And with a green and yellow melancholy,
She sat like Patience on a monument,
Smiling at grief.

Sebastian, who is melancholy because he thinks he has lost his sister, finds that the *stars shine darkly* over him and he says he will *bear my evils alone*. Although the play ends happily except for the fate that has befallen Malvolio, Feste's final song has a melancholy tone. It is as if he is reminding the audience that now the entertainment is over, they must return to the humdrum cares and concerns of ordinary life.

Describe, decide, divide

- ? Describe one incident or exchange which demonstrates the theme of chaos and order.
- ? Who in the play experiences true melancholy, and who is being indulgent?
- ? Divide this circle up into pieces of pie which represent the relative importance of the themes as you see them. Are there any themes you want to add?

treat yourself to a break before you get some style

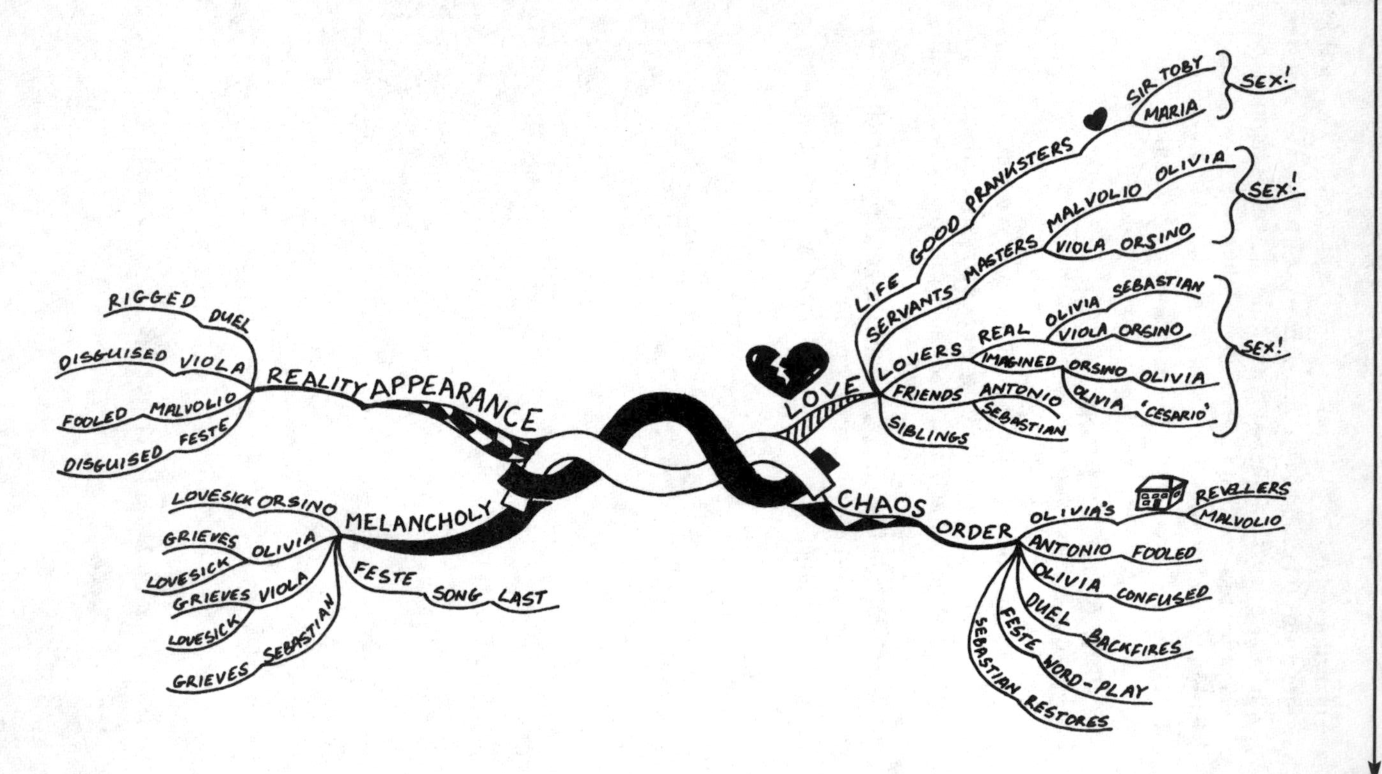
LOVE
LIFE
GOOD
PRANKSTERS
SIR TOBY
MARIA
SEX!
SERVANTS
MASTERS
MALVOLIO
OLIVIA
VIOLA
ORSINO
SEX!
LOVERS
REAL
OLIVIA
SEBASTIAN
VIOLA
ORSINO
IMAGINED
ORSINO
OLIVIA
OLIVIA
'CESARIO'
SEX!
FRIENDS
ANTONIO
SEBASTIAN
SIBLINGS
CHAOS
ORDER
OLIVIA'S
REVELLERS
MALVOLIO
ANTONIO
FOOLED
OLIVIA
CONFUSED
DUEL
BACKFIRES
FESTE
WORD-PLAY
SEBASTIAN
RESTORES
APPEARANCE
REALITY
RIGGED
DUEL
DISGUISED
VIOLA
FOOLED
MALVOLIO
DISGUISED
FESTE
MELANCHOLY
LOVESICK
ORSINO
GRIEVES
OLIVIA
LOVESICK
GRIEVES
VIOLA
LOVESICK
GRIEVES
SEBASTIAN
FESTE
SONG
LAST

LANGUAGE, STYLE AND STRUCTURE

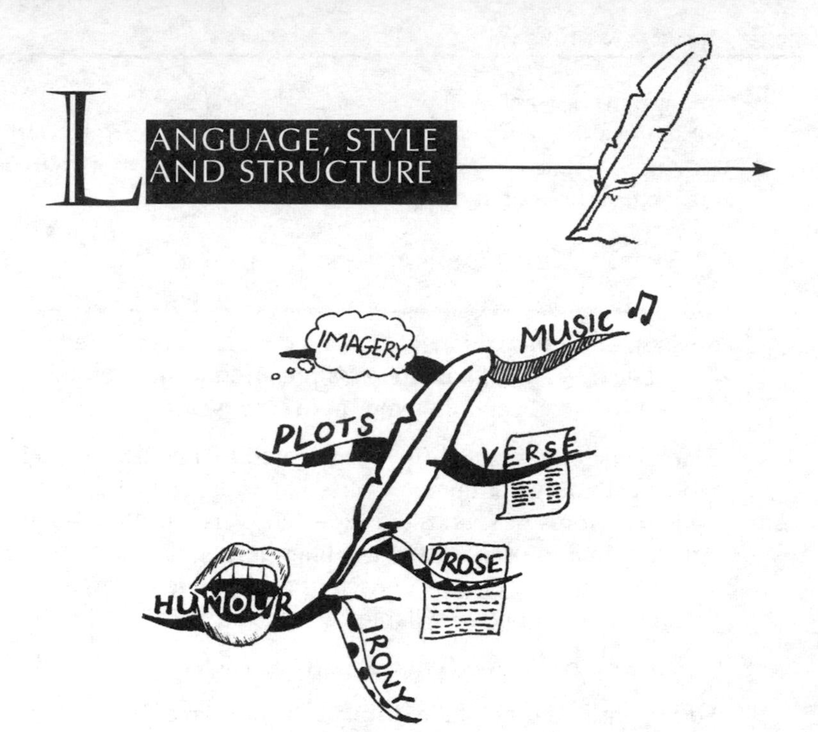

Can you think of times when you use different types of language? For example, you probably use words with friends that you would not use with a teacher or a parent. In the same way, Shakespeare varies the language he gives his characters according to who they are, who they are speaking to, and what they are speaking about. Note that Feste makes his living by the way he uses words. *Twelfth Night* is written in a mixture of verse and prose.

Prose

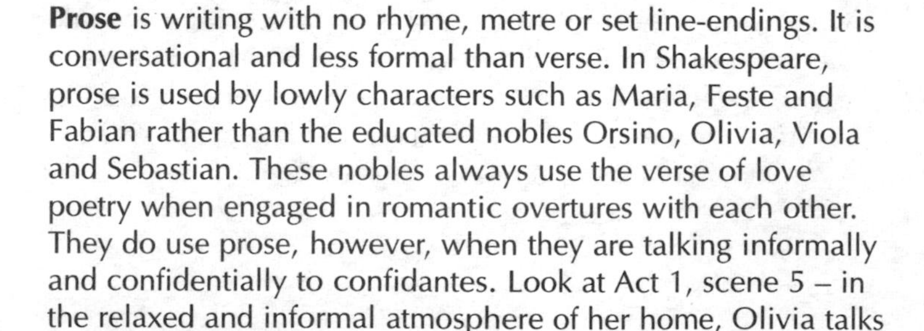

Prose is writing with no rhyme, metre or set line-endings. It is conversational and less formal than verse. In Shakespeare, prose is used by lowly characters such as Maria, Feste and Fabian rather than the educated nobles Orsino, Olivia, Viola and Sebastian. These nobles always use the verse of love poetry when engaged in romantic overtures with each other. They do use prose, however, when they are talking informally and confidentially to confidantes. Look at Act 1, scene 5 – in the relaxed and informal atmosphere of her home, Olivia talks to Feste, Malvolio and Viola/Cesario in prose. As the tone changes to become a romantic appeal, Olivia and Viola/Cesario talk in verse. ✪ Why do you think Sir Toby and Sir Andrew speak in prose rather than verse, even though they are nobles, not commoners?

Verse

Shakespeare's formal language, called **blank verse**, is rather like poetry. Verse is Shakespeare's preferred form of writing about love – the central theme in *Twelfth Night*.

Blank verse has a regular rhythm created mainly by the way words with different numbers of syllables are joined together and how words or sounds are repeated. Verse also has a tighter structure than prose. Most of the lines are regular, and in Shakespeare, they usually consist of five **iambic feet**. An **iambus** is a foot of two syllables:

If mu/sic be/the food/of love,/play on, (Act 1, scene 1, line 1).

You might find it helpful to think of this mnemonic – Iam-*buses* always come in twos.

✪ How many syllables are there in this line? Now choose a speech in which the verse looks regular, and tap the beat while saying it aloud. How many beats are there to each line? Now choose a speech written in prose. Does it have the same, consistent number of beats?

A further feature of Shakespearean verse can be found in his treatment of the last two lines of many of the scenes – you will see that they rhyme. The 'rhyming couplet' as it is called, placed at the end of a scene, neatens things up and is a useful way to warn the audience that the scene is ending. Rhyming couplets can also be used to give a note of finality at the end of some speeches. Look at the way Orsino dismisses Viola/Cesario in Act 5, scene 1, lines 166–7. Two rhyming couplets are grouped together to emphasise Viola's romantic passion in Act 5, scene 1, lines 133–6.

Imagery

Imagery is the use of words to create pictures, or images in the viewer's or reader's mind. Imagery makes what is being said more effective, can make an idea more powerful, and can help create a mood. You will find examples of imagery on almost every page of Shakespeare. Images of seas and shipping, nature and the hunting of animals are often used in *Twelfth Night.*

Just as we are interested in what might be found by space probes on Mars, people living in the age of Sir Frances Drake, Sir Waler Raleigh and the Spanish Armada were fascinated by maritime exploration. Maria's comment about Malvolio reflects this interest: *He does smile his face into more lines than is in the new map with the augmentation of the Indies* (Act 3, scene 2, lines 74-6).

There is much talk of events at sea and an image of shipping is used as a **metaphor** (description of a thing as if it were something essentially different but also in some way similar) for the coming and going of characters in Act 1 scene 5 (lines 94–5). Maria politely asks Viola to leave by comparing her with a ship about to set sail. Viola replies that she will remain anchored where she is a little longer, addressing her as a *swabber* (deck scrubber):

MARIA (showing Viola the way out) *Will you hoist sail, sir?*
VIOLA *No, good swabber, I am to hull here a little longer.*

✪ Can you find a similar example used by Viola in Act 3, scene 1 (between lines 70–80)?

Images of nature and hunting are used to create the soft atmosphere of love and to consider the wooing of an unsecured romance. For examples of this, look at Orsino's speeches in the opening scene, and at his words again in the earlier part of the final long scene. Similar images are used by Sir Toby as they observe Malvolio from the box-tree. Shakespeare also uses Greek mythology to illustrate something about his characters. Sebastian is compared to Arion, who safely escaped drowning by riding on a dolphin's back. Viola's lips are compared to those of the goddess Diana. Viola hopes Sebastian has gone to Elysium – the Greek heaven.

The device of **personification** (description of something abstract as if it were a person) is used by Viola in Act 2, scene 4 between lines 109–17. Write down the quality that she personifies here:

Test yourself

- ? Find an example of a rhyming couplet, and think about what effect it achieves.
- ? Which characters always speak in prose and why?
- ? Look at the language used in the love scenes. Why are these scenes written in verse?

take a break between two 'I's

Irony

Irony occurs when the opposite of what is meant is said, or when something turns out in the opposite way to that which is intended. Although Shakespeare uses irony in many of his plots and as a device in the language he gives to many of his characters, he largely forgoes its use in *Twelfth Night* in favour of humorous intrigue. Perhaps this is because the use of irony tends to be more powerful when used in a serious way.

Examples of irony in *Twelfth Night* include Orsino's advice to 'Cesario' that he should choose a woman younger than himself, and the way that Olivia asks for 'mad' Malvolio to be cared for by Sir Toby. ✪ In view of Sir Toby's idea of caring for Malvolio, why is Olivia's request ironic?

Although there is relatively little ordinary irony, the text is rich in **dramatic irony**. This arises when the audience, and perhaps some of the characters, know something that other characters do not. The most obvious use of dramatic irony in *Twelfth Night* occurs in the way that only the audience knows Viola is disguised as Cesario and that she loves Orsino. The audience is also privy to the private thoughts of Sebastian, Malvolio when he reads 'Olivia's' letter, and when Sir Andrew is meant to fight 'Cesario'. Revelations made to the audience and not the other characters help to unify the play and give it much of its entertainment value.

This technique of directly informing only the audience of private thoughts is called an **aside**. A **soliloquy** is a longer speech delivered by a character alone on stage. Soliloquys usually feature more serious thoughts. In *Twelfth Night* the soliloquy is used by Olivia (Act 1, scene 5, lines 278–88), Viola (Act 2, scene 2, lines 17–41), and Malvolio in the box-tree scene (Act 2, scene 5). ✪ Write in the spaces who speaks the soliloquys in Act 3, scene 4 ...., and Act 4, scene 3 ....

Structure

In literature, structure refers to the framework for piecing the parts of the work together. It is the see-saw of contrasting plots that provide the play with a unified structure. Feste is also a unifying influence as he is the only character to have a significant exchange with almost all the other characters. He links parts of the play through his musicianship and he looks on but stands apart, an observer of the human condition.

Act 1 sets the scene, introduces the main characters, and the main plot concerned with love. Act 2 develops the main plot, introduces the sub-plot which focuses on the commoners, reveals more about the characters, and the relationships between them. Acts 3 and 4 mainly develop the comic sub-plot concerning Malvolio and introduce an element of farce in the form of the duel. The play reaches its climax with all the muddles in Act 5 before the main plot and the sub-plot are resolved and the loose ends are tidied up. It is almost possible to separate the main and sub-plots in *Twelfth Night*, because they are largely developed in alternating scenes. Again Feste has a role here in dipping in and out of both plots which helps them to gel.

Music and atmosphere

Twelfth Night can be considered as a musical. In the tradition of musicals, the thematic content is light and humorous, rather than serious or tragic. The use of music is fitting to a play written about Christmas revels and festivities that was designed to entertain rather than send an audience home in deep thought about the meaning of life.

Music was also very much a symbol of harmony and romance in English poetry and literature during the age of Shakespeare:

If music be the food of love, play on, (Act 1, scene 1, line 1).

It is an important backdrop to the themes of love and melancholy presented in this opening scene, in Act 2, scene 4 and Act 5 as the finale. The music is mainly delivered by Feste, who as we have seen, not only maintains unity in the play by moving freely between different character groups, but also uses his musical talents to provide a further thread of unity.

The plaintive notes of Act 1, scene 1 and the sad song at Act 2, scene 4 so favoured by Orsino help to set the atmosphere of unrequited love in his chambers. Sir Toby and Sir Andrew talk of dancing and merriment in Act 1, scene 3, and Feste is required to sing a love song in Act 2, scene 3 to accompany the drunken revels. This song, *O mistress mine!*, is about acting on feelings now. It also contains words which anticipate the play's happy conclusion, and is the first of several attempts at further songs in the scene which would probably have been chosen by Shakespeare to be recognized by his contemporary audiences.

Feste begins Act 3 by entering the stage *playing his pipe and tabor.* This seems a likely way to settle the audience after an interval. Perhaps he chooses a jolly little song about a robin (Act 4, scene 2) to taunt Malvolio because the bird has a self-important highly coloured breast in an echo of Malvolio's *self-love* and yellow stockings.

The final song brings the audience back down to earth after all the entertainment. It is a song about reality and maturity and drops the light-hearted action of a festive play back in the context of real life.

Setting

The setting, Illyria is thought to be what was Yugoslavia. As with many of Shakespeare's plays, an exotic European setting helped to carry the audience away into the fiction and fantasy that would interest and prepare them for the entertainment ahead. However, there are references to typically English things such as Orsino's *bank of violets* and Antonio and Sebastian arranging to meet at the Elephant Inn. Shakespeare was probably using a combination of exotic setting and images of seafaring and shipwrecks with familiar images that his audience would recognize.

Humour

Twelfth Night shares much with the comedy we enjoy today. The language may have changed, and the type of 'in-joke' has changed over four centuries, but puns (plays on words) have always raised a laugh. Shakespeare takes particular advantage of every opportunity to use puns in *Twelfth Night.* For example, Orsino chooses to take mention of the *hart,* a male deer, to talk of his own aching *heart* (Act 1, scene 1); Sir Andrew thinks Maria's surname is 'Accost' when Sir Toby invites him to 'accost' her (Act 1, scene 3); a drunken Sir Toby mishears Olivia asking him how his *lethargy* (laziness resulting from drunkenness) has occurred so early in the day, and understands her to be referring to *lechery* (Act 1, scene 5). Feste plays with the meaning of words several times at the beginning of Act 3, scene 1. ✪ Look at the first 20 lines of this scene and see if you can understand his manipulations. You will achieve better marks is you can recognize and comment on puns and some of the other characteristics of comedy listed here:

- make the audience laugh or feel happy
- silliness, such as girls dressing up as boys

- confusions which are eventually resolved
- unlikely co-incidences or happenings
- one or more characters are the butt of the jokes
- puns or plays on words
- audience knows more than some or most of the characters (dramatic irony)
- usually a happy ending - no one dies; multiple marriages
- the assumption that 'goodies' won't be harmed.

Over to you

? Tick any of the statements above that you think apply to *Twelfth Night*. Think of an example in the play for each of the statements you have ticked.

? Find the lines in Feste's song *O mistress mine!*, (Act 2, scene 3) that foreshadow the play's conclusion.

? Which characters are responsible for developing the comic elements in the play, and how do they do it?

now take a break from the fun before a running commentary

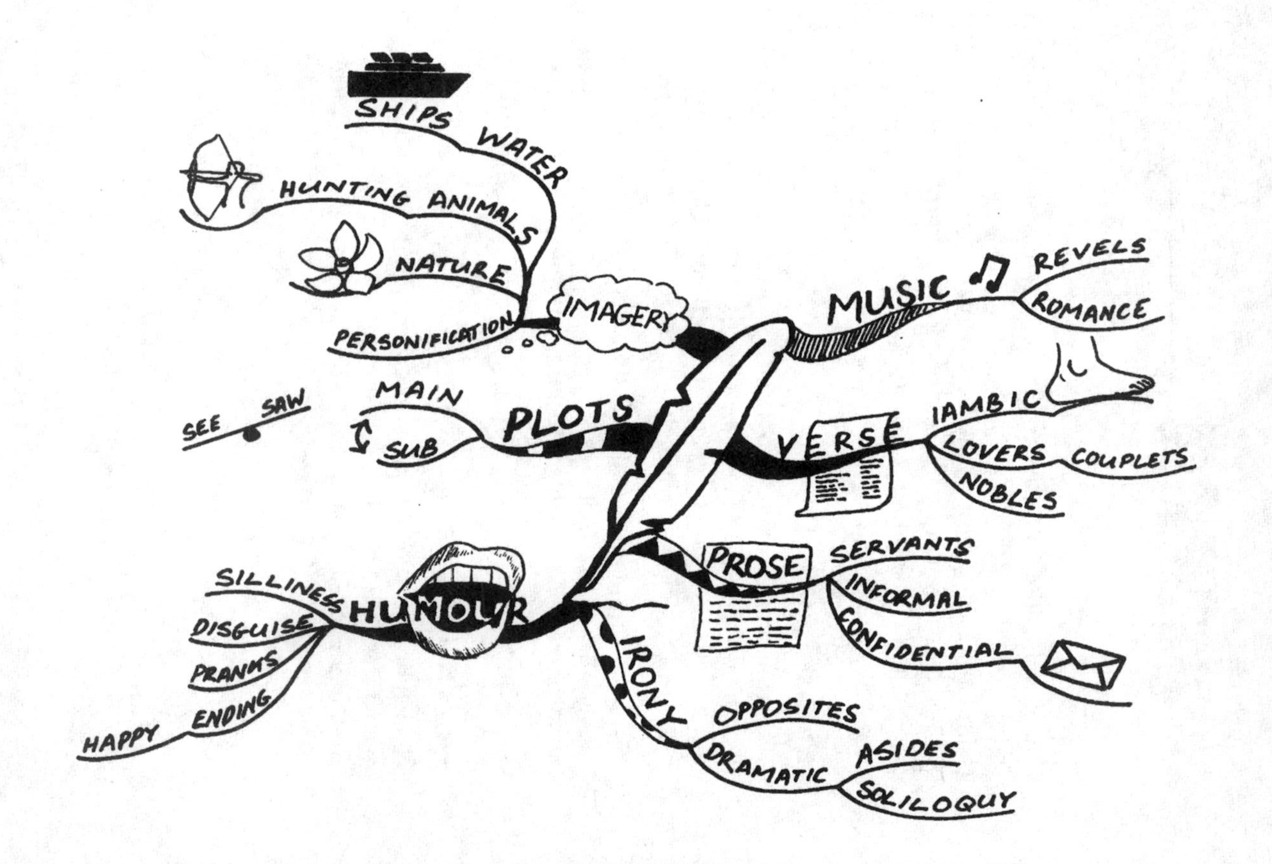
SHIPS
WATER
HUNTING
ANIMALS
NATURE
PERSONIFICATION
IMAGERY
MUSIC
REVELS
ROMANCE
MAIN
SUB
PLOTS
SEE
SAW
VERSE
IAMBIC
LOVERS
COUPLETS
NOBLES
PROSE
SERVANTS
INFORMAL
CONFIDENTIAL
SILLINESS
HUMOUR
DISGUISE
PRANKS
HAPPY
ENDING
IRONY
OPPOSITES
DRAMATIC
ASIDES
SOLILOQUY

The Commentary looks at each scene in turn, beginning with a brief preview which will prepare you for the scene and help with last-minute revision. The Commentary comments on whatever is important in the section, focusing on the areas shown in the Mini Mind Map above.

ICONS

Wherever there is a focus on a particular theme, the icon for that theme appears in the margin (see p. x for key). Look out, too, for the 'Style and language' icons. Being able to comment on style and language will help you to get an A in your exam.

You will learn more from the Commentary if you use it alongside the play itself. Read a section from the play, then the corresponding Commentary section – or the other way around.

QUESTIONS

Remember that when a question appears in the Commentary with a star ✪ in front of it, you should stop and think about it for a moment. And **remember to take a break** after completing each exercise!

Act 1, scene 1

- Orsino speaks of his unrequited love for Olivia.
- Orsino learns that Olivia is concerned only with mourning her brother.

Orsino speaks of his unrequited love for Olivia (lines 1–23)

Music plays as Count Orsino, ruler of the imaginary place Illyria, enters the stage with his attendant Curio and his other courtiers. Music creates the right tone to speak of love rather than affairs of state. Orsino opens with some of Shakespeare's most famous lines as he wallows in his unrequited love for the Countess Olivia:

If music be the food of love, play on,
Give me excess of it, that, surfeiting,
The appetite may sicken, and so die.

Orsino is so lovesick that he says he wants more of the music that makes him feel romantic so that he might become tired of both the music and the troubled romance. He compares the sound of the music dying away to the transient sweet smell of wild violets. He decides he has heard enough and considers the *high fantastical* nature of love. He says that like the sea, love consumes and makes everything worthless in its passion. ✪ Look closely at the images Orsino uses in this scene and judge whether you think he is truly in love.

Curio tries to take Orsino's mind off the subject by suggesting going hunting. He does this in the form of a question, as would be fitting to a servant. Distractedly, Orsino asks what they would hunt, and misunderstands Curio's mention of the male deer called a 'hart', with its homophone (word which sounds the same but is spelt differently) 'heart' – showing that he is not to be distracted so easily. He adds that from when he first saw Olivia he thought she purified the air. It is interesting that he should say this because the air in Shakespeare's London would have been polluted by the stench and disease caused by a lack of sewers, drains and waste disposal such as we now take for granted. It is a great compliment, although to us it does not sound like one. He compares himself and his desire for Olivia to a hart hunted by his own dogs ever since.

Valentine, an apt name for a messenger of love, arrives with news of Olivia.

Orsino learns that Olivia is concerned only with mourning her brother (lines 24–42)

Valentine explains that Olivia would not see him. Instead she sent a message with her maid to say that not even the air will see her face properly for seven years. She will wear a veil, behave like a nun and cry salty tears every day to keep alive the memory of her dead brother.

Orsino admires Olivia for having such sentiments towards a brother. He goes on to surmise that if she feels such love for a brother, what she will feel towards a lover when her mourning ends will be very much greater. He imagines himself lord of her *liver, brain, and heart,* the vital organs which control all passion and feeling. The very idea so appeals to him that he again thinks of flowers and shady bowers where he may languish in his romantic dreams.

By the end of this scene we know the key strand of the plot around which all further developments will revolve. Although we have not met Olivia we have been given a fair picture of her, and so we have been introduced to two of the main characters. These two are also at the top end of the social scale – they are count and countess, part of the titled, wealthy upper class. The natural images at the end of the scene are presented in a rhyming couplet.

Act 1, scene 2

- Details of shipwreck – Viola survives but her brother is missing.
- Viola learns of Orsino and Olivia.
- Viola plans to serve Orsino.

Details of shipwreck – Viola survives but her brother missing (lines 1–21)

In another part of Illyria, Viola talks to the sailors she was shipwrecked with. She says she thinks her brother is in *Elysium* – the heaven of Greek mythology. With hope she asks the sailors if they think there is any chance that he survived. The captain points out that she herself is very lucky to have survived, and supplies some detail of the wreck. As Viola and some other people clung to another boat, the captain saw Sebastian (who is not yet named) bravely bind himself to a ship's mast and drift away on the waves. Viola is comforted by the possibility that Sebastian may be alive, and rewards the captain with some payment.

Viola learns of Orsino and Olivia (lines 22–41)

Viola wants to know more about where she has been washed up and learns from the Captain who is a native of Illyria, that Orsino is governor and a truly noble man. The compliment to the Count gives the audience permission to accept Orsino as a worthy character and prepares the ground for Viola to fall in love with him.

Viola and the Captain have a good gossip about Orsino's romantic hopes. Viola gleans the information that Orsino is unmarried but that a recent rumour suggests that he wants to marry Olivia. The Captain tells Viola that Olivia's father died a year ago, left her in her brother's protection, but that he has also died, leaving the fair lady so upset that she will now see no men.

Viola plans to serve Orsino (lines 41–65)

On hearing this and having also lost a brother, Viola decides that she is not yet ready to reveal who she is but would like to serve Olivia. The Captain points out that this would be difficult to arrange because Olivia will see no one. Viola then declares that the Captain seems trustworthy and she asks him to help her maintain a male disguise so that she may serve Orsino instead. She points out that she can sing and make music but that she has other intentions. Just as she has shown interest in Orsino's marital status, so it is now implied that she may see him as a future husband.

The scene closes with another rhyming couplet in which the captain promises to keep Viola's identity secret. We have been introduced to the next two important characters in a way which mirrors scene 1. Viola will be a key character and so will Sebastian. Just as we do not meet Olivia in scene 1, we do not meet her future lover, Sebastian in this one. Already the play has been given a kind of order and symmetry.

Try this

? Concentrate on the images used by Orsino in scene 1 and list them under the following headings:

music	food	flowers	animals	other

? Describe what we know of Olivia so far.

? How sincere do you think Orsino's love and Olivia's mourning are?

now you've met the nobles take a break before you meet the lowly

Act 1, scene 3

- Olivia's maid Maria reprimands Olivia's uncle, Sir Toby for his debauchery.
- Sir Andrew Aguecheek flirts with Maria.
- The two lords discuss Sir Andrew's hopes of winning Olivia, and exchange more sexual innuendoes.

Olivia's maid Maria reprimands Olivia's uncle, Sir Toby for his debauchery (lines 1–40)

Sir Toby's irresponsible view of life is apparent immediately – he says *care's an enemy to life,* meaning that his niece, Olivia, should stop mourning her brother so deeply. Maria clearly has sufficient status in Olivia's household that she is able to comment on the behaviour of her mistress's kinsman. She lets us know that Sir Toby displeases Olivia by staying out too late and drinking heavily.

She prepares us for meeting Sir Andrew Aguecheek, *a foolish knight,* who has hopes of wooing Olivia. Sir Toby defends his friend as courageous and wealthy, but the witty Maria points out that he will fritter away his fortune quickly. Not to be put off, Sir Toby lists his accomplishments as a musician and linguist. Maria counters them with complaints of the cowardice suggested by his name – the ague was a kind of fever which produced shivering. Combined with 'cheek' the impression is of a quivering face, such as might accompany a cowardly type of person. 'Aguecheek' was also an expression used to describe a pale, lean face.

With the characteristic charm of a cheery drunk, Sir Toby claims to be drinking Olivia's health. He says every man should drink to her until he spins round or rolls head over heels, like what was probably a kind of toy, a *parish top.* He greets his friend about whom they have been speaking, as *Agueface,* perhaps as a kind of insulting joke between friends.

Sir Andrew Aguecheek flirts with Maria (lines 41–76)

The two men greet each other in the manner of drinking buddies. All three then talk in a good-humoured way, with Sir Andrew wishing to know Maria better. Sir Andrew's dull-wittedness shows in his failure to pick up on Sir Toby's invitation to *accost* Maria, thinking he refers to her surname. Both men speak a sexual innuendo in a private remark, or aside, to the audience. This would have raised quite a laugh in a Shakepearean audience, who would understand the joke more easily than a modern one. The sexual joking continues with a comparison between Sir Andrew's sexual ability and calling at a bar to drink.

Note that these characters, although titled, are lowly and lacking in the noble qualities of those we have met or heard of in the opening two scenes. As is fitting to their characters, they speak in ordinary everyday bawdy prose, in contrast with the articulate verse of the virtuous and educated characters to whom we have been introduced in the first two scenes.

The two lords discuss Sir Andrew's hopes of winning Olivia

Sir Andrew again demonstrates his lack of intelligence in his conversation with Sir Toby when they talk of wine and the effect that eating beef has on the wits, or intelligence. Sir Andrew, the supposed linguist, saying he will go home, fails to understand Sir Toby's use of the French word for 'why'. This shows the audience what a dullard he is. He says he wishes he had spent as much time learning languages as he has spent on sport and merry-making. Sir Toby makes a play on the word *tongues* to mean languages, understanding it as tongs for curling the hair. A dirty joke follows in which Sir Andrew's near baldness may be completed by a visit to a prostitute, from whom he may catch a disease which will make the rest of his hair fall out.

Continuing on a more serious note, Sir Toby persuades his friend to stay and court Olivia, assuring him that Orsino has no chance of winning her. Sir Andrew needs little persuasion - the idea of *masques and revels* is enough to tip the balance. They talk of Sir Andrew's prowess as a dancer of kickshawses, the galliard, back-trick, coranto, and jig. He, of course, thinks he dances very well and is flattered by Sir Toby who enjoys making fun of him. He says he should not hide his talents and that his fine legs must have been destined for dancing. Commenting on how good his legs look in stockings, Sir Andrew is foreshadowing (warning of things to come) use of the yellow stockings in which Malvolio will look so ridiculous. The two leave the stage to continue their revels.

Act 1, scene 4

◆ Orsino sends Viola/Cesario to woo Olivia on his behalf.

Back in Orsino's court we learn that Viola, in her disguise as Cesario, is very much in favour with the melancholy count. She has become his bosom friend in just three days. Viola continues to gather information about the count in a way that builds on earlier hints that she is looking for a husband and Orsino is on her shortlist. She is satisfied to learn that the Duke is constant in his affection and that the favour he shows towards her will continue.

Orsino then speaks privately to Viola in her disguise. He tells her that she knows all his secrets, and wants her to woo Olivia on his behalf. He tells her not to allow Olivia to turn her away, and to insist on seeing her. The Duke wants Viola/Cesario to declare his love again, because 'his' youthfulness fits 'him' well for the purpose. Ironically, Orsino even points out how 'Cesario's' youth makes 'him' appear quite feminine, as if he is attracted to her but foiled by the disguise. A few courtiers are ordered to accompany Viola/Cesario, and then Orsino says they should all go because he prefers to be alone – the inference is that he wants to be alone because he is so lovesick. The Duke's final encouragement is that if Viola/Cesario is successful in this mission 'he' should live freely and enjoy the Duke's money and possessions. This, of course, foreshadows the ending of the play when these two become engaged.

Viola/Cesario undertakes to carry out the mission, but adds as an aside, in her true gender, for the ears of the audience only, that this is a difficult task because she herself would like to become Orsino's wife.

Act 1, scene 5

◆ Feste, Olivia, Malvolio introduced.
◆ Olivia is given news of Viola/Cesario's visit.
◆ Viola/Cesario woos Olivia.
◆ Olivia falls in love with Viola/Cesario.

Feste, Olivia, Malvolio introduced (lines 1–93)

The scene shifts again – to Olivia's house. Just as scene 3 began with Maria scolding Sir Toby, so this scene begins in the same way. This time the stop-out is Feste the clown, a servant kept to amuse the countess. He does not say where he has been, or what he was doing. Neither does he seem very worried that Olivia will be angry with him for his absence. He soon shows himself to be quick-witted as he makes several jokes out of misunderstanding things that Maria has said to him. She advises him to have a good excuse ready to give Olivia.

Olivia is more hurt than angry with Feste. It is his task then to give us some of the light chatter befitting a comedy, as he shows us how he will win his way back into her favour. Feste is quite cheeky, since he chooses to understand her dismissal of him, the fool, as a dismissal of herself. He talks truisms (statements that are obviously true) in the form of nonsense and sets about proving who is the fool by the use of logical argument. He finds his own way of saying that Olivia is mourning her brother too deeply.

At this stage we have seen Olivia, surrounded by attendants tolerating the cheeky Feste. She is clearly not as mean-spirited as her steward (chief servant), Malvolio as we soon see. On being asked what he thinks of Feste, his first words are whinges that Olivia puts up with him only because she is sick with mourning. He complains that Feste is not a very good fool compared to others, and that he needs an indulgent audience to be able to perform. Olivia reproves his disposition and tells him in effect, to 'lighten up'. The joke, as we will soon see, will turn on Malvolio.

Olivia is given news of Viola / Cesario's visit (lines 94–160)

Maria enters with news of Viola/Cesario's visit. We have been prepared for this, are expecting it, and know the nature of the mission and of Viola/Cesario's feelings for Orsino which are private to her and the audience. Olivia guesses that Viola/Cesario has been sent by Orsino, and sends Malvolio to use any excuse to get rid of 'him', believing Sir Toby to be inadequate for the task.

Her suspicions are correct, because an extremely drunk Sir Toby arrives on stage to make the audience laugh. Probably experiencing indigestion from drink and burping to illustrate his name, he blames pickled herrings and then mis-hears Olivia, who asks him how he has become drunk so early in the day. Having used the word 'lethargy' he chooses to hear the word 'lechery', before he staggers off stage. Olivia enjoys a little more of Feste's banter. Clearly she has forgiven him his absence and sends him off to look after Sir Toby.

Malvolio then returns, perplexed that he has not been able to get rid of Viola/Cesario, who seems *fortified against any denial* to be given access to Olivia. Her curiosity aroused, Olivia draws a description of Viola/Cesario out of Malvolio. ✪ In the light of what happens next, do you think Olivia is secretly interested in having suitors or that she thinks this youth will not be difficult to deal with? Or do you think she might just be bored? She decides to hear out yet another entreaty from Orsino and she and Maria put on their veils to assume a public display of mourning.

Viola/Cesario woos Olivia (lines 161–277)

Viola/Cesario begins a flowery speech without knowing which of the two women is Olivia. They banter as Viola/Cesario keeps asking who Olivia is. To the amusement of the audience, and deflating Olivia's ego somewhat, Viola/Cesario says she doesn't want to waste the excellent speech she has been composing on the wrong person. Olivia digs for information about this youth who reveals little and has been admitted because she wants to *wonder* at rather than *hear* Viola/Cesario.

Using images of ships sailing and mooring, Viola/Cesario declines Maria's invitation to leave. Viola/Cesario says that what she has to say is private, and Olivia, becoming more and more curious about this youth, dismisses her attendants. Viola/Cesario asks to see Olivia's face. Olivia, comparing herself to an unveiled painting, complies, and Viola/Cesario compliments her on her beauty and says she should have children in order to pass it on. This statement of course assumes that she should end her mourning and marry Orsino.

The two continue, Viola/Cesario professing Orsino's love, and Olivia fairly praising him, but saying she cannot love him. Because she herself is in love with Orsino, Viola can say quite sincerely that she cannot understand how Olivia can be so untouched by his attentions.

Olivia, by now, is quite smitten with this Viola whom she takes to be a man, and wants to know more about 'him'. Satisfied that Viola/Cesario is eligible, despite her secretiveness, Olivia says she wants to hear no more of the count but Viola/Cesario may call again on the pretext of telling her how he takes the news. Viola/Cesario will take no money for her efforts and leaves.

Olivia falls in love with Viola / Cesario (lines 278–301)

Left alone, Olivia thinks aloud about Viola/Cesario. She says how attractive she finds 'him', and wonders at how quickly a person can fall in love. In a display of quick and determined thinking, she calls Malvolio and sends him after Viola/Cesario to return a ring (which Viola did not give) as an excuse to make sure Malvolio actually stops her. She instructs Malvolio to ask Viola/Cesario to return the next day to hear her reasons. What she actually wants is to see Viola/Cesario again. She ends the scene with the observation that her heart might rule her head, and in a rhyming couplet accepts that what will be will be.

Now try this ...

- ? How does Feste prove to Olivia that she, not he, is the fool?
- ? What impression do you have of Viola at this point in the play?
- ? Write a brief paragraph announcing the shipwreck for *The Illyria Times.*

now take a break before running on

Act 2, scene 1

- Sebastian mourns his twin sister Viola.
- Antonio becomes Sebastian's devoted friend.

Sebastian mourns his twin sister Viola (lines 1–30)

The scene shifts to somewhere else in Illyria. We are introduced to two new characters. Sebastian is with Antonio the sea-captain who has saved him from the shipwreck. Sebastian does not wish to depress Antonio with his low spirits since he is so unhappy. However, he perceives a friend to whom he can talk and so tells Antonio for his benefit, and that of the audience, who he is. He adds that he has a twin sister, the Viola who we have come to know in Act 1, and that he believes she has drowned. He talks of their likeness, explains that he has his mother's gentle and feminine nature which makes him prone to shedding unmanly tears for his sister.

Antonio becomes Sebastian's devoted friend (lines 31–43)

Sebastian does not invite Antonio's offer to serve him, but adds for our benefit that he is going to Orsino's court. In a private word with the audience, Antonio says that he has enemies at Orsino's court which should prevent him from going there – he does not say why. He decides however, that he has such a passion for his friend that he will take the risk and go anyway.

It is apt that this scene should follow the previous one, because we are immediately able to make the connection that not only is Sebastian alive, but he will become a suitable husband for Olivia, since she has fallen in love with his twin sister. That he is bound for Orsino's court helps to make us want to know what will happen next, and how the love-muddles will be resolved. ✪ Why does this scene echo Act 1, scene 2?

Act 2, scene 2

- Viola realizes that Olivia has fallen in love with her.

In this second short scene the pace of events is increasing. We have also been introduced to all the characters and know what is on their minds. Malvolio catches up with Viola/Cesario and returns what he believes to be Orsino's ring. The pompous and high-handed manner he adopts does little to endear Malvolio to the audience. Viola/Cesario plays along with Olivia's deception, and when left alone, ponders the meaning of it.

Viola realizes that Olivia has fallen in love with her Cesario, feels sorry for her because no relationship can take place between them, and sees the mischief caused by her disguise. She muses on the gentle and impressionable nature of women, and the hopelessness of the love triangle in which she loves Orsino, he loves Olivia and Olivia loves Viola/Cesario. Ending with a rhyming couplet, Viola recognizes that she cannot influence these complications which time alone can unravel.

Act 2, scene 3

- Sir Toby, Sir Andrew and Feste enjoy revels.
- Malvolio tells them off.
- Maria explains her plan to make fun of Malvolio.

Sir Toby, Sir Andrew and Feste enjoy revels (lines 1–85)

This humorous scene is set late at night when the revellers have been having fun. Sir Toby and Sir Andrew joke about their lateness and justify it with a twisted logic. They call for more wine, Feste joins them and they gossip about Malvolio and decide to have a sing-song. Sir Toby wants Feste to sing a drinking song, a song of the good life. Sir Andrew misunderstands and thinks they want a hymn. They tip Feste and he sings a song which foreshadows events to take place later in the play. The group is so drunk, they decide to sing a really loud and rousing song. This brings Maria to them. As usual she brings warnings of Olivia's displeasure, but she makes no difference – they carry on *caterwauling*.

Malvolio tells them off (lines 86–120)

A stern and angry Malvolio enters to ask the revellers if they have no respect for Olivia and her status, whether they have no manners or decency or consideration for other people to make such a noise so late. He claims that Olivia has told him to say that unless Sir Toby can take his bad behaviour elsewhere, he is not welcome to continue living in her house, even if he is family.

The three respond drunkenly by being cheeky, making light of the reproach and singing more songs. They repeat their request for more wine in front of Malvolio and remind him of his relatively lowly position in the household. Fortified by alcohol, they clearly feel no threat. Malvolio exits after telling Maria she should produce no more drink if she has any respect for her mistress. ✪ How does Malvolio's entrance and stern manner change the atmosphere?

Maria explains her plan to make fun of Malvolio (lines 121–84)

After Malvolio leaves, they grumble about him. Sir Andrew, rather ridiculously, says Malvolio should be challenged to a duel in an exchange which hints at the duel to come later in the play. Always keen to lead the less than intelligent Sir Andrew on, Sir Toby offers to write the challenge for him. But Maria, by far the cleverest of them, reveals that she has an idea to make fun or *common recreation* as she calls it, of Malvolio. Like a dog sensing weakness, she explains that Malvolio is vain and big-headedly always thinks he is right and also thinks everybody likes him. It is this part of his character, she says, that she means to exploit as a joke.

She says that the next day she will leave love-letters for him to find which appear to have been written by Olivia about him. This will be easy because her handwriting is very like Olivia's. The others are delighted with this plan and are instructed by Maria that they are to hide near these abandoned letters so that they may overhear anything Malvolio may say about them. Sir Toby praises his future wife and as the scene ends, encourages Sir Andrew to send for more money. Clearly he has little, but Sir Toby continues to suggest that all will be well if he is successful with Olivia.

Act 2, scene 4

- Lovesick Orsino asks Viola/Cesario about 'his' own romance.
- Feste sings a love song.
- Viola/Cesario tries to make Orsino receptive to a new love.

Lovesick Orsino asks Viola about 'his' own romance (lines 1–41)

In an echo of the opening scene of the play, Orsino is again languishing in unrequited love for Olivia. He wants music again, not light dance music, but old serious music to soothe his lovesick soul. Viola/Cesario tells him that Feste is the singer of that particular song – a detail that perhaps Orsino has failed to take in due to his distracted state.

Orsino orders the tune to be played while Feste is found to come and perform it for him. This has the effect of setting the scene for a discussion about love and provides the right tone for a romantic interchange between Orsino and Viola/Cesario who will be declaring her love for him, although Orsino will not realize it.

Little realizing that he is addressing a girl and that she is in love with him, a fact which of course, the audience knows, he invites Viola/Cesario to remember him if he should find himself lovestruck. ✪ What is ironic about this? Wallowing in his lovesick way, a state which he seems to rather enjoy, he goes on to say that he is so true in his love that he can concentrate on nothing but Olivia. Viola comments that the tune fits the image of Olivia very well.

Orsino realizes that although Viola/Cesario is young, 'he' is perhaps in love too. As Orsino asks questions about this imaginary woman, Viola answers as truthfully as she can, saying the woman has similar looks and age to Orsino.

Orsino then starts a 'man to man' observation about lovers that would be considered sexist in modern times. He says that the woman should be younger than the man or he will not be faithful, because the emotional commitment of men is less reliable than women's. He adds that men can only stay constant if a woman is younger, because women lose their looks as they age. Viola reluctantly agrees.

Feste sings a love song (lines 42–77)

Orsino says that the simple old song Feste is about to play is sung by people who knit, weave and sew. It is pure and innocent in its subject matter. In effect he is leading us into the song as a character might in any musical. The sad song is all about unrequited love so deep that the lover dies of it – a very fitting theme for the over-dramatic Orsino. Feste again shows pride and independence of spirit by refusing the tip Orsino tries to give him. As he leaves he makes a wise wish for Orsino that he may be open to what happens to him, in order to make the most of life.

Viola/Cesario tries to make Orsino receptive to a new love (lines 78–124)

Left alone, Orsino asks Viola/Cesario to go and pay his suit to Olivia once again. Being realistic, and probably also harbouring her own romantic hopes towards Orsino, Viola challenges Orsino to face up to the fact that she is simply not interested. She adds, in a way that the audience but not Orsino knows is referring to herself, that if a woman loved Orsino as he loves Olivia she would deserve to be told there was no hope.

Orsino flatters himself that no woman could love another as he loves Olivia. He claims that women simply are not capable of such depth of feeling. Viola argues that he is wrong by example. Again, only the audience knows that the example she uses is her own even though she illustrates it with reference to a sibling of her own, tinged with as much reference to her own affection as Cesario for Orsino as she can get away with.

Wanting to know more about this sibling, Orsino is told that this woman hid her love from its object, and pined away for the love of him. In making such sacrifice, she says, women love just as much but do it more quietly than men. Orsino seems to think that this woman should have died for her love in order to prove the point. This prompts Viola to privately lament the death of her brother for a moment before she agrees to woo Olivia on Orsino's behalf once again.

What do you think?

- ? What do you think of Orsino after this scene?
- ? In his thinking aloud at the end of Act 2, scene 1, Antonio speaks in verse, when the rest of the scene has been spoken in prose. Why do you think this is?
- ? What do you think Olivia would have said if she had found out about the plan to ridicule Malvolio?

give yourself a break before some eavesdropping

Act 2, scene 5

- ◆ The pranksters hide and wait for Malvolio.
- ◆ Malvolio falls into the trap.
- ◆ The pranksters enjoy the joke.

The pranksters hide and wait for Malvolio (lines 1–22)

Sir Toby, Fabian, the servant, and Sir Andrew prepare to enjoy the prank they are about to play on Malvolio. They all relish the idea of making a fool of the man who has corrected their wayward behaviour. Maria comes along and tells them to hide in a nearby tree because Malvolio is on his way. She adds that he has been admiring his own shadow which tells us that the trap has already been set and is beginning to work. Malvolio is feeling light-hearted and pleased with himself.

Malvolio's use of his shadow could create a very light-hearted and pleasing image for the audience, and give a lighting technician some fun. Maria puts a letter in Malvolio's path and makes sure we understand that it is an instrument to further ensnare him in the prank.

Malvolio falls into the trap (lines 23–172)

Malvolio enters the stage already reflecting on his good luck. He has begun to re-interpret small details of his dealings with Olivia so that he begins to believe she favours him. As he works through each point, seeing it in a new light, the pranksters whisper to each other so that the audience – but not Malvolio – can hear. Sir Toby and Sir Andrew can hardly contain their horror that he should fantasize about becoming a count or that he could imagine Olivia taking a daytime nap to recover from the passionate love he has made to her.

When Malvolio imagines using new powers to chastise Sir Toby for his drinking and mentions the poor company he keeps in Sir Andrew, they all but shout out and reveal themselves. ✪ How would you organize the stage and direct this part of the play to exploit its humour and dramatic irony to full effect?

Malvolio then finds the letter Maria has left for him. As she has predicted he mistakes her handwriting for Olivia's. He identifies individual letters as hers, choosing those that refer to the private area of a woman's body, probably a Shakespearian trick to make Malvolio talk in an uncharacteristically dirty way. He reads on, and considers the next set of letters, which make no sense. Still, Malvolio manages to persuade himself that because the individual letters are in his name, regardless of the order in which they appear, the letter is for him.

He goes on to read a set of statements and suggestions for how he should behave if he returns the love he thinks he has gained. He resolves to become all the things outlined in the letter, the significant ones being that he should wear yellow stockings with cross-garters (garters crossing at the back of the knee and tied above it at the front). Such a colour would, of course, not be in keeping with anyone in mourning, and both the colour and the cross-gartering were old-fashioned by the time the play was written. ✪ What other things does Malvolio swear to do?

Having fallen into the trap Maria has set for him, Malvolio reads the PS (post script) she has mischievously added to the letter – that if he loves Olivia he should smile in her presence – a habit he is not noted for. He ends his fantasy with a declaration of intent to smile and leaves the stage. He has fallen for the prank, and is being thoroughly made fun of.

The pranksters enjoy the joke (lines 171–200)

The pranksters have enjoyed every second of Malvolio's humiliation. Fabian says he would not part with a huge pension to have missed it and Sir Toby feels he could marry Maria for her cleverness in devising such a good laugh. This anticipates their marriage at the end of the play. The three men congratulate Maria, and Sir Toby notes that when the joke is over, Malvolio *must run mad.* ✪ Do you think he means mad with the sorrow of a broken heart or mad with anger?

Just in case we missed Malvolio's resolutions and to give us an indication of what to expect next, Maria repeats the key points of her letter, which Malvolio can be counted on to act out. She says he will wear yellow tights and cross-garters, a colour and fashion which Olivia hates. His smiles will be at odds with how melancholy his mistress is feeling.

Act 3, scene 1

- Viola/Cesario and Feste talk philosophy.
- Viola/Cesario talks love with Olivia.

Viola/Cesario and Feste talk philosophy (lines 1–90)

Viola/Cesario is on her way to see Olivia on Orsino's behalf once again. She meets Feste, who jokes with words in his wise fool's way. The nature of the exchange, in which Viola is quite capable of holding her own, is a kind of logic game to begin with. It leads on to talk about the nature of words and how they present philosophical problems in trying to understand human reasoning. Since Feste has entered the stage playing music, and the conversation is of general interest rather than bearing any relation to the play, perhaps Shakespeare had meant there to be an interval. If you think about it, you can just imagine a high-spirited audience returning to the auditorium to be further entertained. These two and their banter would allow the crowd to settle down for the rest of the action.

We come back to the subject of the play as Feste continues to comment on domestic politics, suggesting that husbands are fools, and Olivia will have one of these when she marries. Noting that foolishness can be found everywhere, and it visits both Orsino and Olivia, Viola brings the banter to an end. She tips Feste for his wit, laments her own love for Orsino, and takes the hint that she may see Olivia if she produces a larger bribe.

Viola/Cesario comments on Feste's foolish wisdom, powers of observation and general cleverness as Sir Toby and Sir Andrew enter. Viola/Cesario again shows how well she can hold her own in any company as Sir Toby invites her in and they pick up the imagery of boats once again.

The pranksters against Malvolio again listen on as Viola/Cesario is presented to Olivia and flatters her with compliments. They know from Maria that Olivia is smitten with Viola/Cesario and it is with reluctance that they leave the two alone.

Viola / Cesario talks love with Olivia (lines 91–161)

Left alone, Viola/Cesario courteously represents Orsino's suit. Olivia asserts her lack of interest in the count, and quickly asks Viola/Cesario to court her, saying she would rather that *Than music from the spheres.* She goes on to admit to her deception of sending the ring with Malvolio as a pretext to make Viola/Cesario return. She adds that the feelings she has for Viola/Cesario are making her shamefully forward.

Viola/Cesario fails to respond to Olivia's appeals, and using the imagery of animals, hunters and prey, Olivia rescues her wounded pride by saying that even if she is rebuffed, she is proud to have fallen for a fine man rather than one less worthy. Still Viola/Cesario tries to press Orsino's suit but is dismissed. Even so, Olivia cannot resist one more attempt to court Viola/Cesario. They exchange witty words about not being who or what they think each other to be (lines 135–9).

Viola/Cesario's continued resistance has the effect of making Olivia keener than ever. First she ponders this in an aside and then she makes a direct appeal to Viola/Cesario in a passionate confession of her love. Viola/Cesario avoids a direct response to this appeal but replies with an explanation that only the audience will understand – that she will never give her heart to any woman. She adds that she will not return to press her master's suit again. Olivia asks Viola/Cesario to return, with the lie that perhaps she will learn to love Orsino, when what she really wants is to see Viola/Cesario again.

Olivia's confession (from line 144) and the remainder of the scene is love poetry in the form of a series of rhyming couplets, showing the eloquence both characters are able to command to fit the occasion.

Act 3, scene 2

- Sir Andrew is set up for a duel.
- The pranksters joke at the expense of others.

Sir Andrew is set up for a duel (lines 1–50)

In contrast to the serious love-talk of the previous scene the mischief-makers are busy again. Sir Andrew tries again to leave Olivia's house, only to be persuaded by Fabian and Sir Toby that she is in love with him. Using several references topical to the time, they claim that Olivia's preference for Viola/Cesario is a diversion from where her real affections lie. They cunningly develop this idea by suggesting that Sir Andrew has almost missed his chance with Olivia by not being bold, and that he will have to find his way back into her favour either by some act of bravery or by appropriate sweet-talk.

Sir Andrew does not trust his ability as a sweet-talker and so allows himself to be persuaded to challenge Viola/Cesario to a duel to impress Olivia. Sir Toby tells him to go and write the challenge in the most confrontational way he can, and they will deliver it.

The pranksters joke at the expense of others (lines 51–80)

As soon as Sir Andrew has left the stage, Fabian and Sir Toby have a laugh at his expense. They do not seriously believe that the duel will take place – they think Sir Andrew is a coward and Viola, disguised as Cesario, too gentle a character to fight.

Their mischief-making continues as Maria enters the stage with news of Malvolio. She says that they will laugh themselves into stitches when they see Malvolio because he has fallen for everything she has written in the fake letters from Olivia, is acting ridiculously and wearing the very old-fashioned yellow stockings, cross-gartered. She adds that he smiles so much that her mistress will probably hit him! They all leave the stage to go and laugh at Malvolio.

Test your recall

? Choose the right word:

- Having been three *days/weeks/months/years* married to her ... (Malvolio, Act 2, scene 5, line 43).
- She will keep no *dog/husband/budgie/company,* sir till she be married ... (Feste, Act 3, scene 1, lines 31–2).
- I have one *mind/house/lover/heart,* one bosom, and one truth. (Viola, Act 3, scene 1, line 155).

? Explain the arguments Sir Toby and Fabian use to persuade Sir Andrew to stay another month.

? See if you can complete this crossword. The answers are on p. 73.

Across

1 Several of the characters are afflicted with this.
6 Another name for a prank.
7 Viola/Cesario and Sir Andrew are set up for this.
9 A lover and ruler.
10 What Viola says Patience did on a monument.
12 Place where everything happens.
13 Malvolio is one of these.
14 A way of referring to the audience.
15 The name of someone in disguise.
17 Type of tree in Twelfth Night.

Down

1 Name of a key character.
2 Harp-like instruments popular at the time.
3 What Viola/Cesario says to Olivia?
4 What the pranksters do behind a tree.
5 Another name for Christmas.
8 Shortened word for beginning.
11 A servant in the play.
14 Orsino sends Viola/Cesario to do this to Olivia.
16 Twelfth Night ___ What You Will.

Act 3, scene 3

- Antonio looks after Sebastian.

In this scene, we observe that Sebastian is coming closer to the main action. The purpose of the scene is also to demonstrate Antonio's friendship and generosity which will soon be apparently betrayed in one of the comic misunderstandings.

We learn that Antonio is so devoted to Sebastian that he has accompanied him to Illyria to protect his friend from harm because he knows the land well. He explains that he will not go sight-seeing with Sebastian because he was involved in a fight at sea with Orsino's men. Although he was provoked, he did not kill Orsino's men, but will be remembered by them with hostility. Antonio says he will go ahead to the Elephant, an inn where they will stay and order some food while Sebastian looks around. Antonio very generously gives Sebastian his purse in case he wants to treat himself at the shops. ✪ What do you think of Antonio's extreme generosity towards Sebastian?

Act 3, scene 4

- Malvolio makes a fool of himself.
- Fabian and Sir Toby advance the duel.
- Viola/Cesario has trouble with Olivia and Sir Andrew.
- Antonio comes to Viola/Cesario's rescue, but is arrested.
- Antonio thinks Sebastian is ungrateful.

Malvolio makes a fool of himself (lines 1–140)

In this long scene, various strands of the plot start to come together in farcical chaos. An Elizabethan audience would have a great time watching each misunderstanding develop at the expense of one character or another. Note how this scene deals only with the many comic deceptions for which Shakespeare has been busy laying the foundations. The theme of love between the true lovers is on ice for a little longer.

First we learn from Olivia that she cannot leave Viola/Cesario alone – the countess has sent for her beau again and is plotting ways to the heart of the woman she thinks is a man. She sends for Malvolio because, with the way she is feeling, she wants his sober and serious company. This of course is Shakespeare's way of preparing us for a laugh – Maria warns her mistress that Malvolio is *tainted in's wits.* Malvolio appears in his ridiculous costume smiling in an awkward and uncharacteristic way.

He points out that the cross-gartering is cutting off his circulation, but dismisses the discomfort since he thinks it will please Olivia. She of course thinks he has turned a little mad, and caringly suggests that he goes to bed to recover. Malvolio thinks she is inviting him to share her bed, and you can almost hear the bawdy jeers from the audience as he agrees with enthusiasm.

Malvolio continues to quote lines from the letters he thinks Olivia has written to him. By her replies it is clear to everyone except the poor steward himself that she has no idea of what he is talking about. Olivia goes off to meet Viola/Cesario, and leaves instructions that Sir Toby should see to Malvolio with special care. What he actually receives as *special care*, however, is not quite what she had in mind!

Olivia and Maria leave the stage, and Malvolio, sinking ever deeper into the trap, muses on more of the instructions he has been given in the fake letters. These relate to the way he is to be stubborn, argumentative and surly towards Sir Toby and the other servants. Sir Toby, Fabian and Maria enter and enjoy goading Malvolio as if he is possessed by the devil. He proudly leaves the stage in a manner firmly abusive of the three, whom he considers shallow and beneath him. In a game with the audience, Shakespeare makes Fabian comment that the scene would hardly be believable if it were to be acted out in front of him – as indeed it is.

The three decide that they must lock Malvolio up before he discovers he has been made the victim of a prank. They fear no reprisal from Olivia because they have made her think he is mad already, and they want to prolong the joke for their own amusement.

Fabian and Sir Toby advance the duel (lines 141–96)

Next it is Sir Andrew's turn to be the butt of the joke. The silly knight appears with his challenge to Viola/Cesario, and Sir Toby and Fabian read it at his request. Although the note is full of insults and challenges, it does not say why the challenge has been issued. Sir Toby and Fabian compliment Sir Andrew on the note and how it avoids saying anything which could be considered a breach of the peace, while Fabian privately comments to the audience that it makes little sense.

Sir Toby tells Sir Andrew he will deliver the note and, on being told that Viola/Cesario is nearby visiting Olivia, suggests that he should lie in wait and be ready to draw his sword and behave in a menacing manner. This action, Sir Toby says, may frighten Viola/Cesario more than actual violence. He, of course, knows full well that Sir Andrew will need all his limited courage even to do this, and it is the anticipated spectacle that the cowardly knight will make of himself that the mischief-makers (and the audience) want to enjoy.

As Sir Andrew leaves the stage, Sir Toby says to Fabian and Maria that he will not deliver the note because it is too pathetic to make a personable young man such as Viola/Cesario take it seriously. He resolves instead to deliver the challenge in person which will give him the opportunity to invent for Sir Andrew the courage, bravery and foul temper which should scare his opponent so much that on seeing each other the duellists will do all their fighting simply with fierce looks.

Viola / Cesario has trouble with Olivia and Sir Andrew (lines 197–302)

Olivia undeterred by Viola/Cesario's lack of interest, cannot help herself. She declares her passion again and that she knows she is too forward. She asks Viola/Cesario to wear a picture pendant of her as a love token and is met with a request that her passion be directed at Orsino instead of herself. She asks Viola/Cesario to visit her again the next day.

As Olivia leaves the stage, Sir Toby and Fabian re-enter. They tell Viola/Cesario that a formidable Sir Andrew is lying in wait for her, they do not know why, and she must prepare herself. Understandably, she at first thinks they must be mistaken since she has a clear conscience. Sir Toby continues to make Sir Andrew sound terrifying and says that he is so incensed with hatred for her that he will stop at nothing except death.

Closer to the truth than she realizes, Viola/Cesario says that this must be the kind of man who picks fights for the sake of it. Sir Toby says seeking protection from Olivia will not help either, so she must prepare to meet her enemy. Viola asks Sir Toby to find out what she has done to so offend her aggressor, and seeks more information of Fabian. Fabian shows that he is just as clever with words as Sir Toby when he says that this is the most fearsome opponent a person could have, despite appearances which suggest the opposite. Viola/Cesario states that she makes no claims to be a fighter and does not care who knows it. ✪ How do you think she feels at this moment?

At another stage entrance, Sir Toby appears with Sir Andrew. He is similarly engaged in frightening Sir Andrew with tales of Viola/Cesario's fighting prowess. This frightens Sir Andrew so much that he says he will give Viola/Cesario his horse if she will just forget the whole thing. Pretending to do so, Sir Toby takes the horse for himself, and tells Viola/Cesario that Sir Andrew is still spoiling for a fight simply because he has sworn to do so. He adds that she will not be hurt, and then returns to Sir Andrew to tell him a similar lie. Both no doubt, trembling with fear, they draw their swords.

Antonio comes to Viola / Cesario's rescue, but is arrested (lines 303–30)

Antonio appears at just the right moment although neither Viola/Cesario or Sir Andrew have been in any real danger. Antonio says he will fight for Viola/Cesario who he takes to be Sebastian. In another quick-moving part of the action, Orsino's officers arrive. Viola/Cesario and Sir Andrew agree to forget the fight, and a last laugh is exploited out of Sir Andrew's repeat of his promise to give Viola/Cesario his horse, to appease 'his' anger.

The officers move to arrest Antonio who laments the situation he is in because of Sebastian. Still devoted to him, however, he adds that he is more upset that he can no longer serve his friend than he is for his own fate and regrets that he needs his purse back.

Antonio thinks Sebastian is ungrateful (lines 331–86)

Viola/Cesario, as Sebastian's twin knows nothing of the purse, but in her gratitude for being saved from Sir Andrew, offers half of her own money. Antonio cannot believe his ears even as Viola/Cesario says she hates ingratitude as if to explain her own lack of obligation towards this man she has never seen.

In his misery at what he sees as a betrayal, Antonio goes on to explain that he rescued his friend and served him devotedly. He ends with a lament for the ingratitude of Sebastian, whom he names, as he is led away. Viola in an aside, has heard her twin's name mentioned, and realizes what has happened although she can hardly allow herself to hope her brother is still alive.

As Viola leaves the stage, Sir Toby comments to Fabian and Sir Andrew on that *dishonest, paltry boy,* who appears to them as an ungrateful coward. No longer scared, but still full of 'hot air', Sir Andrew says he will go and teach Viola/Cesario a lesson after all. Fabian and Sir Toby go to watch, knowing that little will happen.

Look it up in Act 3, scene 3

- ? What does Olivia say she would give up rather than let Malvolio lose his wits (line 63)?
- ? How many men does Sir Toby tell Viola that Sir Andrew has killed (line 232)?
- ? What is the name of Sir Andrew's horse (line 279)?

take a break before some more mistakes

Act 4, scene 1

- Olivia's servants mistake Sebastian for Viola/Cesario.
- Olivia pleases Sebastian by mistaking him for Viola/Cesario.

Olivia's servants mistake Sebastian for Viola/Cesario (lines 1–44)

Just as the previous scene ends with Viola/Cesario being mistaken for her twin brother Sebastian, so this scene opens with Sebastian being mistaken for Viola/Cesario. Feste cannot believe his ears – Sebastian pretends not to know that he is being sent for by Olivia. Feste presses him to give an answer he can take to Olivia, and Sebastian tips him in the hope that he will go away.

Shakespeare then picks up the thread left at the end of the previous scene. Sir Andrew, Sir Toby and Fabian enter. Sir Andrew, made brave by his friends' company and by his knowledge that Viola/Cesario is no fighter, hits Sebastian. This sibling however, is keener to defend himself and strikes back – another turn of the plot which would have an Elizabethan audience howling with laughter. Feste leaves, vowing that he will tell Olivia what has happened, adding that he would not like to be either of them when she finds out that her darling is being assaulted by her own servants and kin.

Perhaps because he has a shock at Sebastian's response to his threat, Sir Andrew says he will tackle his opponent at law rather than in a fight, even though he struck the first blow. Sir Toby then gets a response he little expects – Sebastian breaks free of his grip and draws his sword. Just as Sir Toby prepares to fight Sebastian, whom he thinks very impudent, Olivia arrives on the scene.

Olivia pleases Sebastian by mistaking him for Viola/Cesario (lines 45–65)

An angry Olivia orders Sir Toby to put down his sword, calls him an *Ungracious wretch*, with no manners, and tells him to keep out of her way. She apologizes to Sebastian, whom she also mistakes for Viola/Cesario.

As the knights and Fabian leave Olivia and Sebastian together, Olivia elaborates on her apology to Sebastian, asking him not to take the assault too seriously. She invites Sebastian to go to her house and laugh about the *fruitless pranks* that Sir Toby has been involved in before adding, on a romantic note, that Sir Toby was responsible for first bringing them together.

Because Olivia has called him by Viola's false name Cesario, Sebastian does not suspect that his sister may also have survived the shipwreck, although he realizes some mistake has occurred. Obviously attracted to Olivia, he wonders to himself and the audience in an aside, what good luck has befallen him. Is he mad or dreaming? Either way he hopes the mysterious favour Olivia shows him will continue. They leave the stage to indulge in sweet talk.

Act 4, scene 2

- Feste visits Malvolio disguised as a priest.
- Feste talks to Malvolio as himself and the priest.

Feste visits Malvolio disguised as a priest (lines 1–70)

The pranksters are busy again. Maria tells Feste to dress up as a priest called Sir Topas. As she goes to fetch Sir Toby, Feste dresses to fit the part, though he comments that he is too short and not thin enough to be entirely convincing. With more of his philosophical word-play Feste prepares himself for his encounter with Malvolio. He is egged on by Maria and Sir Toby who remain hidden from Malvolio who is locked in a darkened room – the traditional treatment for mad people.

Feste approaches Malvolio, who quickly asks him to go to Olivia. Feste, continuing the joke at Malvolio's expense and, to the delight of Maria and Sir Toby, pretends to think Malvolio is possessed by the devil, as a priest might. Malvolio protests to the 'priest', but Feste keeps up the deception and pretends to test Malvolio's sanity. He does this by saying the only true darkness is ignorance, not the room in which Malvolio is kept.

Malvolio challenges 'Sir Topas' to test him with any logical argument.

He is answered with a request to know what Pythagoras's theory was concerning reincarnation. By now the audience knows that Feste will twist whatever answer Malvolio gives to suit his purposes. In saying that he respects Pythagoras, but does not agree with his theory that a bird may carry the soul of a grandmother from a previous life, Malvolio is dismissed by Feste with having given the wrong answer, much to Sir Toby's delight.

Where Malvolio cannot hear them, Maria comments that the priest disguise has not been necessary to have the desired effect, and Sir Toby tells Feste to approach Malvolio as himself. He wants Feste to find a way for Malvolio to be released from the joke because he is worried that Olivia will be even more angry with him than she is already if she finds out how they have treated Malvolio.

Feste talks to Malvolio as himself and the priest (lines 71–128)

As the other two leave the stage, Feste sings, as himself, in front of Malvolio, that Olivia loves someone else. Malvolio, probably realizing this, asks Feste for light, pen and paper. Jesting with words again and pretending alternately to be himself then Sir Topas, Feste teases the prisoner. As Sir Topas, he pretends to exorcize the devil in Malvolio, as himself he clowns about, eventually agreeing in a song, to fetch pen and paper.

Act 4, scene 3

- A confused Sebastian tries to make sense of his good luck.
- Olivia presses Sebastian to become formally engaged.

A confused Sebastian tries to make sense of his good luck (lines 1–21)

Alone on the stage, Sebastian tries to make sense of what is happening to him. He is delighted to be so favoured by Olivia, but wonders if either she or he is mad. He has been to the Elephant Inn to find Antonio, and hears that Antonio has not only been there but has been trying to find him. Antonio's whereabouts are still a mystery, however. Sebastian wishes he could find Antonio because he could perhaps give him some good advice about this development with Olivia.

Sebastian carries on thinking aloud – he knows there is something strange about Olivia's demonstrations of affection for him, and trusts it to be true. At the same time, the situation is so pleasing to him, that he again wonders if he, or Olivia, is mad. He reasons, however, that she would not be able to receive information from her servants and issue instructions to them so efficiently if she was mad.

Olivia presses Sebastian to become formally engaged (lines 22–35)

Still smitten with Viola/Sebastian, Olivia is a woman of action and wastes no time in proposing to Sebastian since she thinks he has changed his ways and started to take an interest in her. She brings a priest onto the stage with her and tells Sebastian that if he is serious about her, she wants a formal engagement to take place in the nearby chapel. She explains that this will stop her feeling jealous and insecure about his affection for her. She goes on to say that she is happy for the engagement to be kept secret until he is ready for a marriage fitting to her status to take place. Sebastian readily agrees to go ahead with the betrothal, and swears to be true.

Act 5, scene 1

- Feste uses his wits to extract money from Orsino.
- Antonio mistakes Viola/Cesario for Sebastian and complains about her to Orsino.
- Viola/Cesario denies her engagement to Olivia. Orsino is furious.
- Sir Andrew accuses Viola of assaulting him and Sir Toby.
- Two sets of lovers sort themselves out.
- A humiliated Malvolio is released – the others celebrate.

This very long scene, the only one in Act 5, ties up all loose ends, pairs lovers off appropriately, and clears up all misunderstandings. Everyone is a winner except Malvolio.

Feste uses his wits to extract money from Orsino (lines 1–45)

The final scene of the play begins with more foolish word-play as Fabian wants to see the letter from Malvolio that Feste should be giving to Olivia. As Orsino and his followers enter the stage, Orsino greets Feste, who talks in opposites, saying that enemies are better than friends because friends lie and enemies tell the truth. This prepares the way for some of the revelations that are about to be made.

Orsino enjoys Feste's wit and gives him a tip. Feste is quick to use words to further entertain Orsino who agrees to tip him again. Pushing his luck, Feste tries to turn the ritual into a counting game and tries for a third tip. This time, Orsino resists but adds that he may feel generous again if Feste fetches Olivia to him.

Antonio mistakes Viola / Cesario for Sebastian and complains to Orsino (lines 46–98)

Antonio and his guards enter the stage, and Viola/Cesario tells Orsino that he rescued her. It is important to realize that she means Antonio rescued her from the fight with Sir Andrew not the shipwreck. Orsino says he remembers Antonio being glorified for wrecking his best ship with a very shoddy one of Antonio's.

The guards further comment on his brave exploits, and say they caught him with no money, brazenly fighting in the streets of Illyria. Viola/Cesario speaks up for Antonio saying how kind he was to intervene in a brawl on her behalf, although he made strange accusations towards her, and must have been a little mad. Orsino asks Antonio why he has been so foolish as to return.

Antonio insists that he is not a thief or a pirate, although he admits to having been an enemy of Orsino's. He explains that he was drawn there out of a desire to protect and serve *That most ingrateful boy,* Viola/Cesario, whom he naturally mistakes again for the Sebastian he rescued from the sea. He finishes with the illustration of Viola/Cesario's ingratitude – that she would not return the purse he had given her only thirty minutes earlier.

Viola/Cesario, does not know what he is talking about, and it then comes to light that some mistake has been made. Antonio says that he and Viola/Cesario have not been separated for a minute in three months, and Orsino points out that Viola/Cesario has been with him for the last three months. Still they have no explanation for the mix-up.

Viola / Cesario denies her engagement to Olivia. Orsino is furious (lines 99–169)

Olivia enters to enquire of Orsino what she can do for him since she will not give him what he wants. She also accuses Viola/Cesario of breaking 'his' promise. Olivia will not allow Orsino to speak – she is angry and wants an explanation from Viola/Cesario. Since Viola/Cesario will not speak when her master wishes to, Olivia snubs Orsino.

Orsino, who on seeing Olivia a few lines earlier has said *now heaven walks on earth,* then turns nasty. In his pique at her refusal to accept him, he says he is tempted to kill her, but since he know she prefers Viola/Cesario, whom he also holds dear, he will kill Viola instead, out of spite. ✪ What do you notice about the imagery Orsino uses in this passage (lines 115–29)? Ever faithful, Viola says she will gladly die if it will make her master feel better.

Olivia asks Viola/Cesario where she stands, and hears that Viola/Cesario will do anything for Orsino whom she loves above everything and everyone, adding that she wants to be punished for getting in the way of Orsino's amorous ambitions. Since they are all still at cross-purposes, Olivia believes herself to have been betrayed by her fiancé, and calls for the priest who betrothed them. To Viola/Cesario and Orsino's surprise she calls Viola *husband,* and explains Viola/Cesario's behaviour as a faint-hearted fear of reprisals from Orsino.

Olivia welcomes the priest and tells him that although they had meant the engagement to be a secret for the time being, she now needs him to say what he has witnessed. The priest duly states that he has contracted Olivia and Viola/Cesario in an *eternal bond of love,* with an exchange of rings two hours earlier. ✪ Do you think it is strange that no mention of names formed part of this ceremony?

Then it is Orsino's turn to feel betrayed. He tells Viola/Cesario that he wonders how much more deceitful she will be when she is a more mature adult. He adds that she is so low that she may betray herself in her betrayal of others, and uses a crisply final rhyming couplet (lines 166-7) to emphasize his intention never to see her again. ✪ What impression is conveyed when he calls her a *dissembling cub* (lying fox cub)?

Sir Andrew accuses Viola / Cesario of assaulting him and Sir Toby (lines 170–205)

Sir Andrew intrudes upon this melodrama to add the comic dimension once again. He demands a surgeon for himself and for Sir Toby because Viola/Cesario has beaten them both up. Again Viola/Cesario protests that she was set upon by them and has harmed nobody. Sir Andrew insists she has drawn blood from his head, and would have suffered injury herself from Sir Toby if he had not been drunk at the time. The two revellers clown about as they leave the stage to attend their wounds.

Two sets of lovers sort themselves out (lines 206–74)

At last Sebastian arrives on the scene to make sense of all the misunderstandings which centre on his sister, whom he does not recognize because she is dressed as a man. He begins by apologizing to Olivia for hurting Sir Toby in self-defence, and mentions the vows they have just made. Meanwhile everyone else is looking on in amazement, as voiced by Orsino:

> *One face, one voice, one habit, and two persons!*
> *A natural perspective, that is and is not.*

Sebastian then spots Antonio and is delighted to see him. Antonio is similarly surprised to see the twins together. Olivia is relieved to have an explanation for the inconsistent behaviour displayed by her lover.

Sebastian then turns his attention to his twin. He states that he has no brother, that he did have a sister who has drowned and asks Viola what relation she is to him. In reply, she says that she also believed her brother to have drowned and asks Sebastian if he has come as a ghost to haunt them. He says that if she were his sister he would cry with joy to see her again.

In order to confirm their identities to each other, the twins then exchange information that would only be known to them. They agree that their father had a mole on his forehead and that he died on Viola's thirteenth birthday. Viola then admits that she is indeed Viola in disguise as a man and says she can prove it by taking Sebastian to visit the captain who has her real clothes and who helped her to secure her job with Orsino. She adds that she has been involved with Orsino and Olivia since the shipwreck.

The tone of the scene changes again – the chaotic misunderstandings have been cleared up, and it is time for the love plots to be tidied up. Sebastian addresses Olivia. He confirms her mistake and comments on the way she has been attracted to the twins, and would have been engaged to a woman. Orsino is quick to shift the focus of his romantic interest to Viola. He indicates that he will soon be happy as a result of the revelations, and in a question presented as a statement, asks Viola if she loves him. She replies that all she has said in admiration of him still applies and that she loves him wholeheartedly. Orsino wants to see her in her woman's *weeds* (clothes) and she explains again that the captain has her clothes and is now employed by Olivia in looking after Malvolio.

A *humiliated Malvolio is released – the others celebrate (lines 275–405)*

Olivia calls for Malvolio, and then remembers that his mind has been disturbed. She says that she has been too caught up in her own affairs to think about him. At this moment, Feste arrives with the news that Malvolio is fighting off the devil and has sent her a letter. Feste adds that he meant to deliver the letter earlier that day, but had decided that the letters of mad people do not need to be delivered urgently.

In his characteristic way, Feste reads the letter and rants about madness and wits until Olivia takes it off him and commands Fabian to read it instead. The gist of the letter is that Malvolio is very bitter because he has been wronged by Olivia, who he sees as the person responsible for locking him up in the dark, to be taunted by Sir Toby. He adds that he has her letter commanding him to dress and behave as he has, that he has neglected his duty and does not care what she thinks of him, he has been so *madly-used.*

Orsino observes that the contents of the letter do not seem to be those of a mad person, and Olivia instructs Fabian to fetch Malvolio. While this is being done, Olivia offers to host and pay for Orsino's wedding to Viola. Orsino accepts, releases Viola as a servant, and tells her that since she has done so much for him – despite being men's work as well as beneath her good breeding – that he will marry her.

With both marriages organized at last, Malvolio re-enters the action with accusations of wrong-doing directed at Olivia. He complains that she cannot deny her involvement in the prank because of the handwriting, the form of words which are hers, and the seal. He implores her to tell him why she showed him favour, made him dress ridiculously, smile, and frown on the revellers, and then lock him up for it.

Olivia points out that the letter he thinks was from her is in Maria's handwriting. Olivia then recalls that it was Maria who first told her Malvolio was out of sorts. Realizing that he has been treated unfairly, she promises Malvolio that he shall choose the punishment for the prank when they find out who is responsible.

Fabian volunteers the required information saying first that he hopes it will not spoil the remarkable and happy day they are experiencing. He then explains that he and Sir Toby had taken exception to Malvolio's manner, got Maria to write the letter and followed up the prank for mean fun. He adds that Sir Toby has married Maria to make up for her part in the trick, and that they should all have a good laugh about it rather than seek revenge because Malvolio has treated them as badly as they have treated him. ✪ Is it true that Sir Toby and Fabian dreamed up the prank?

Olivia voices her sympathy for Malvolio, and Feste confesses to having pretended to be the priest who visited Malvolio in his captivity. Feste cannot resist getting even with Malvolio for criticizing him to Olivia earlier in the play. Feeling thoroughly ganged up on, Malvolio leaves the stage swearing to have revenge on all of them. Orsino wants Malvolio to be appeased and make a truce, and he also wants information regarding the captain's whereabouts so that Viola's clothes can be recovered. He says that he and Viola will then be formally betrothed. Just before they leave the stage, he says that they will stay at Olivia's house until then, and that Viola will still be Cesario until she is properly dressed. All the characters exit leaving Feste to sing the last song of the play.

Tie up the loose ends

- ? Do you think that the tidying up of loose ends in the final scene of the play is too contrived or do you find the conclusion satisfactory?
- ? How does Feste's last song put events that have taken place in the play into perspective?

Solution to crossword (p. 58)

1 M	E	2 L	A	3 N	C	4 H	O	L	5 Y
A		Y		O		I			U
6 L	A	R	K			7 D	U	E	L
V		E		8 I		E			E
9 O	R	S	I	N	O		10 S	A	T
L				T		11 F			I
12 I	L	L	Y	R	I	A			D
O				O		13 B	O	R	E
	14 W	E				I			
	O		15 C	E	S	A	R	I	16 O
17 B	O	X				N			R

TOPICS FOR DISCUSSION AND BRAINSTORMING

One of the best ways to revise is with one or more friends. Even if you're with someone who hardly knows the text you're studying, you'll find that having to explain things to your friend will help you to organize your own thoughts and memorize key points. If you're with someone who has studied the text, you'll find that the things you can't remember are different from the things your friend can't remember – so you'll be able to help each other.

Discussion will also help you to develop interesting new ideas that perhaps neither of you would have had alone. Use a **brainstorming** approach to tackle any of the topics listed below. Allow yourself to share whatever ideas come into your head – however silly they seem. They will get you thinking creatively.

Whether alone or with a friend, use Mind Mapping (see p. vi) to help you brainstorm and organize your ideas. If with a friend, use a large sheet of paper and coloured pens.

Any of the topics below could feature in an exam paper, but even if you think you've found one in your actual exam, be sure to answer the precise question given.

CHARACTER

1 Write a CV for Feste, giving evidence of his ability as a fool.
2 How far do you feel the prank against Malvolio is justified?
3 How could Malvolio get his revenge?
4 How likely is it that marriage will improve Sir Toby's character and behaviour?
5 In what ways are Sebastian and Viola similar, or dissimilar, in character?
6 What does Malvolio say about Feste in our first encounter with them, and how does Feste get his own back?
7 Who accuses the revellers of being *idle, shallow things,* and how far is it a fair description of them?

THEMES

1 *... care's an enemy to life.* How far does the play support this belief?
2 How far do you agree with Orsino's advice to Viola about choosing a wife?
3 Which of these lines illustrate which theme?
  - *Is there no respect of place, persons, nor time in you?* (Act 2, scene 3, lines 90–1)
  - *A natural perspective, that is and is not.* (Act 5, scene 1, line 214)
  - *Even so quickly may one catch the plague?* (Act 1, scene 5, line 284)
  - *My stars shine darkly over me.* (Act 2, scene 1, line 3–4)
4 Which of the couples do you think will most enjoy married life?
5 Who is the greater fool, Malvolio, Feste, or Sir Andrew?
6 What is the difference between plot and theme? Give an example from the text to illustrate what you mean.

LANGUAGE

1 What two words does Antonio use to describe the sea in Act 5, scene 1, lines 70–80?
2 Find a rhyming couplet, explain who says it, what it means, and why that character has used it.
3 What effect does putting a comic scene after a more serious one have?
4 Explain the duel plot in your own words.
5 Find out who said each of the following lines, explain what they mean and/or who is being referred to. Only look them up if you really can't remember.
  - *for here comes the trout that must be caught with tickling.* (Act 2, scene 5, lines 21–2)
  - *Now he's deeply in. Look how imagination blows him.* (Act 2, scene 5, lines 41–2)
  - *Some are born great, some achieve greatness, and some have greatness thrust upon 'em.* (Act 2, scene 5, lines 140–1)
  - *a plague o' these pickle-herring!* (Act 1, scene 5, lines 15–16)
  - *And thus the whirligig of time brings in his revenges.* (Act 5, scene 1, lines 73–4)

6 How effective is the metaphor:
She never told her love,
But let concealment, like the worm i'the bud,
Feed on her damask cheek. (Viola: Act 2, scene 4, lines 109–10)

STAGING

1 Make notes on how you would film or stage either Act 3, scene 4, or Act 5, scene 1. It will probably help to divide the scene into 'sub-scenes' (perhaps as the commentary has been organized in this book) and consider them one at a time but as part of a sequence.
2 How would you stage the play to make it as relevant as possible to modern times?

HOW TO GET AN 'A' IN ENGLISH LITERATURE

In all your study, in coursework, and in exams, be aware of the following:

- **Characterization** – the characters and how we know about them (e.g. what they say and do, how the author describes them), their relationships, and how they develop.
- **Plot and structure** – what happens and how it is organized into parts or episodes.
- **Setting and atmosphere** – the changing scene and how it reflects the story (e.g. a rugged landscape and storm reflecting a character's emotional difficulties).
- **Style and language** – the author's choice of words, and literary devices such as imagery, and how these reflect the mood.
- **Viewpoint** – how the story is told (e.g. through an imaginary narrator, or in the third person but through the eyes of one character – 'She was furious – how dare he!').
- **Social and historical context** – influences on the author (see 'Background' in this guide).

Develop your ability to:

- Relate **detail** to **broader content, meaning and style.**
- Show understanding of the author's **intentions, technique and meaning** (brief and appropriate comparisons with other works by the same author will gain marks).
- Give **personal response and interpretation**, backed up by **examples** and short **quotations.**
- **Evaluate** the author's achievement (how far does the author succeed and why?)

Make sure you:

- Know how to use **paragraphs** correctly.
- Use a wide range of **vocabulary** and sentence structure.
- Use short, appropriate **quotations** as evidence of your understanding of that part of the text.
- Use the correct **literary terms** to explain how an author achieves effects with language.

THE EXAM ESSAY

You will probably have about an hour for one essay. It is worth spending about 10 minutes planning it. An excellent way to do this is in the three stages below.

1 **Mind Map** your ideas, without worrying about their order yet.
2 **Order** the relevant ideas (the ones that really relate to the question) by numbering them in the order in which you will write the essay.
3 **Gather** your evidence and short quotes.

You could remember this as the **MOG** technique.

Then write the essay, allowing five minutes at the end for checking relevance, and spelling, grammar and punctuation. **Stick to the question**, and always **back up** your points with evidence in the form of examples and short quotations. Note: you can use '. . .' for unimportant words missed out in a quotation.

Model answer and plan

The next (and final) section consists of a model answer to an exam question on *Twelfth Night*, together with the Mind Map and essay plan used to write it. Don't be put off if you don't think you could write an essay as good as this one yet. You'll develop your skills if you work at them. Even if you're reading this the night before the exam, you can easily memorize the MOG technique in order to do your personal best.

The model answer and essay plan are good examples to follow, but don't learn them by heart. It's better to pay close attention to the wording of the question you choose to answer in the exam, and allow Mind Mapping to help you to think creatively.

Before reading the answer, you might like to do a plan of your own to compare with the example. The numbered points, with comments at the end, show why it's a good answer.

QUESTION

Does Malvolio deserve the treatment he is given?

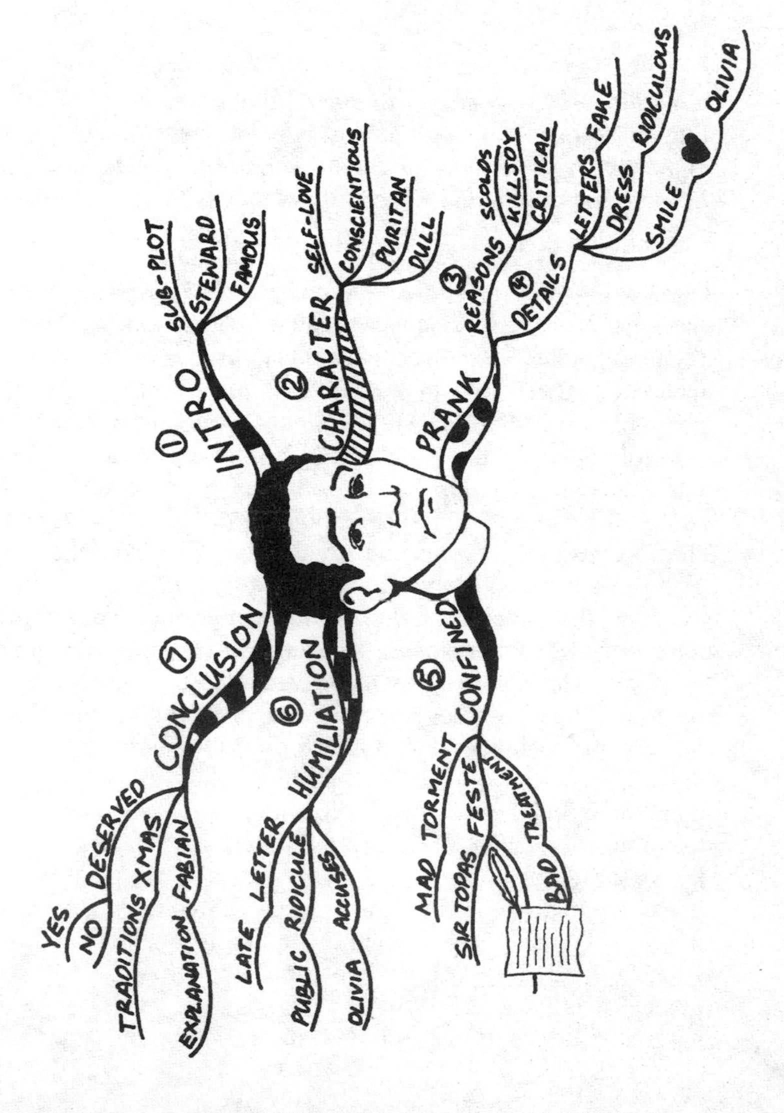

PLAN

1 Intro – context in play.
2 Outline the character of Malvolio.
3 Reasons for playing the prank.
4 Outline the prank.
5 The prank goes too far.
6 Malvolio's humiliation.
7 Conclusion (include reference to festivities)

ESSAY

Malvolio is the steward, or manager, of the countess Olivia's estate. Although he is one of Shakepeare's most famous characters, and perhaps the most memorable in Twelfth Night, he is not part of the main plot. He is, however, the central figure in the play's sub-plot.[1]

Malvolio is first introduced in Act 1, scene 5. He accompanies his mistress who consults him as to his opinion of the clown, Feste. In reply, Malvolio is openly critical of Feste and is then described by Olivia as sick of self-love, meaning that he is a vain and self-centred man. As an easy-going person with a sense of humour, Olivia shows that she is very tolerant of Feste's flaws and is fond of him. She points out that Malvolio is the opposite of generous, guiltless, and free of disposition (lines 85-7) but she could be describing Feste when she lists these qualities as he provides the greatest contrast with the serious and sober steward.[2]

Although Malvolio is a dull person who stands aloof from the group with a superior air, he is almost certainly very good at his job. He is quick to try to break up the party in Act 2, scene 3, when the revellers are having a good time enjoying the seasonal festivities. He claims to be scolding them for making so much noise and revelry in Olivia's house on her behalf, but Shakespeare offers no evidence that she is not tolerant of it – rather it is probably Malvolio's idea of how things should be in her house that makes him say what he does.[3] Either way, Olivia clearly values Malvolio greatly and makes the remark that commends him more highly than any other in the play. It occurs when she is concerned for his mental health and says: 'I would not have him miscarry for the half of my dowry' (Act 3, scene 4, lines 63–4). This comment is very important because it is the greatest measure of how unfairly he is treated.[4]

To teach him a lesson for being, amongst other things, a puritan and a time-pleaser, Maria devises the prank to teach him a lesson by playing to his greatest weakness – his vanity. In league with Sir Toby, Sir Andrew and Fabian, she leaves letters she has forged in Olivia's handwriting for Malvolio to find which will invite him to think that his mistress is in love with him.[5] So flattered by the idea, Malvolio quickly falls into the trap, and lacking a worldly shrewdness, also falls for the rest of the plan. This is for him to smile uncharacteristically and to wear yellow cross-gartered stockings – garments which were not only ridiculously old-fashioned by the time the play was performed, but which had the added joke of being a jolly colour to clash with Olivia's melancholy mood as well as being the colour she detests.[6]

The funniest scene in the play is Act 2, scene 5 in which Malvolio fancies himself married to Olivia, ordering the other characters around. Perhaps because of what they hear about themselves while they are eavesdropping, they devise worse for him.[7]

Obeying the instructions of the prank, Malvolio presents himself in this ridiculous costume to Olivia who, egged on by Maria, thinks he is going mad. Olivia ironically plays into the hands of the pranksters by arranging for Sir Toby to look after Malvolio.[8] Instead of just enjoying the joke they have had, which is embarrassing for Malvolio and mischievous of Maria, they cannot resist continuing to torment the silly steward who is proving to be more of a fool than Feste, the official one. It is when Malvolio is locked up in a darkened room (the treatment for mad people in Shakespeare's day) that the joke seems to go too far. Even then the pranksters taunt him by sending Feste first to pretend he is a priest who will exorcize the devil in Malvolio, and then to fool around as himself.[9]

Feste, who has become involved in the prank only in its later stages, does provide Malvolio with pen and paper to write to Olivia, but he is slow to deliver the letter. By now it is difficult not to feel sorry for Malvolio. His humiliation is almost complete. He has been tricked, humiliated and presumably feels disappointed to lose a new-gained love. When Olivia sends for him and hears his explanation, and the plot is revealed, it is not surprising that Malvolio rushes off-stage making a bitter promise to have revenge on them all.[10]

Whether or not Malvolio has deserved the humiliation he suffers is hard to say. He is certainly a killjoy, and perhaps deserved to be taught a lesson for ruining the fun of others, but the joke does seem to be carried too far. It is also important to remember that this is a Christmas play when people let go and have fun. It may also be the case that there were superstitions and traditions in Elizabethan England to do with warding off evil spirits. Perhaps Malvolio is an exploration of this. At the end of the day we must accept Fabian's explanation as Olivia does, that the prank has been 'sportful malice'. We must conclude: 'If that the injuries be justly weighed/That have on both sides passed', then Malvolio did deserve at least some of the treatment he receives.[11]

WHAT'S SO GOOD ABOUT IT?

1. Good grasp of character's context in play.
2. Apt quotations/sensitively drawn contrast between characters.
3. Perceptive and well-reasoned personal response.
4. Good grasp of issue.
5. Awareness of structure of relationships.
6. Demonstrates thorough knowledge of play, as well as social context.
7. Appreciation of style.
8. Awareness of devices.
9. Ability to argue critically.
10. Strong personal voice and enthusiastic response.
11. Conclusion reveals understanding of historical context, avoids over-simplification.

The essay overall never strays from the question, gives clear well-argued answers and shows a mature overview of play.

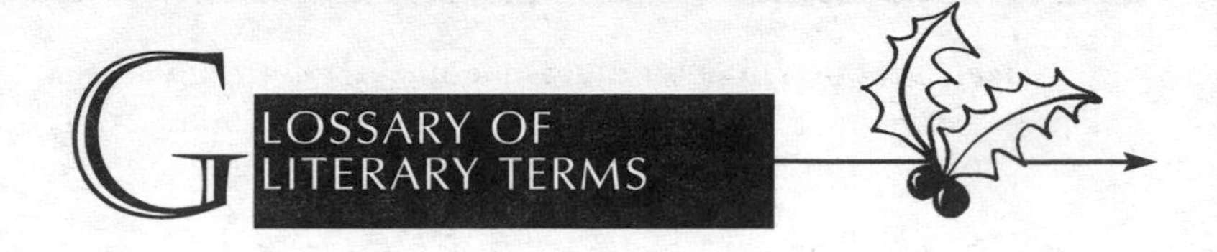

alliteration repetition of a sound at the beginnings of words; e.g. *sweet sound.*

aside a short speech spoken by one character, as if thinking aloud, not meant to be heard by others on stage.

blank verse the kind of non-rhyming verse, with five pairs of syllables to each line, in which Shakespeare usually writes. Also called iamic pentameter.

comedy in Shakespeare, those plays that feature at least some humour, and have happy endings (usually marriages), and no deaths.

context the social and historical influences on the author.

couplet *see* rhyming couplet.

dramatic irony *see* irony (dramatic).

foreshadowing an indirect warning of things to come, often through imagery.

iambic pentameter *see* blank verse.

image a word picture used to make an idea come alive; e.g. a **metaphor**, **simile**, or **personification** (see separate entries).

imagery the kind of word picture used to make an idea come alive.

irony (dramatic) where at least one character on stage is unaware of an important fact which the audience knows about, and which is somehow hinted at; (simple) where a character says the opposite of what they really think, or pretends to be ignorant of the true facts, usually to show scorn or ridicule.

metaphor a description of a thing as if it were something essentially different but also in some way similar; e.g. *Will you hoist sail, sir?* (as if 'Cesario' is a ship).

personification a description of a thing as if it were a person; e.g. ... *O Spirit of love, how quick and fresh art thou* (Act 1, scene 1).

prose language in which, unlike verse, there is no set number of syllables in a line, and no rhyming; the less noble characters speak in prose.

pun a use of a word with two meanings, or of two similar-sounding words, where both meanings are appropriate in different ways.

rhyming couplet a pair of rhyming lines, often used at the end of a speech.

setting the place in which the action occurs, usually affecting the atmosphere; e.g. the coast of Illyria, or Orsino's court.

simile a comparison of two things different in most ways but somehow similar; e.g. ... *my desires, like fell and cruel hounds* (Orsino, Act 1, scene 1).

soliloquy a long speech made by an actor alone on stage.

structure how the plot is organized.

theme an idea explored by an author; e.g. appearance and reality.

viewpoint how the story is told; e.g. through action, or in discussion between characters.

INDEX

Page numbers in bold refer to major character or theme sections.

BUZAN TRAINING COURSES

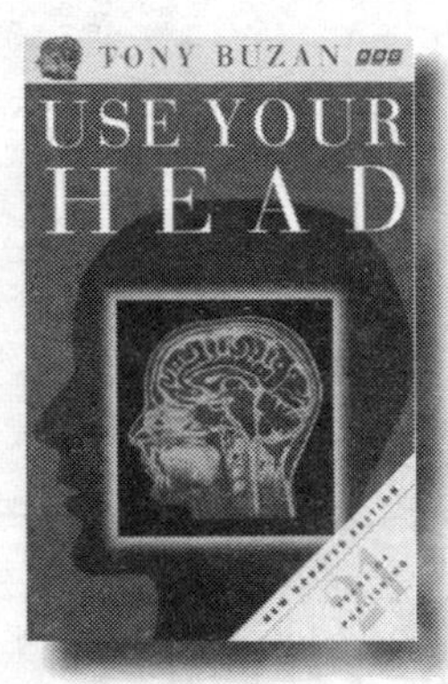

For further information on books, video and audio tapes, support materials and courses, please send for our brochure.

Buzan Centres Ltd, 54 Parkstone Road, Poole, Dorset, BH15 2PX
Tel: 44 (0) 1202 674676, Fax: 44 (0) 1202 674776
Email: Buzan_Centres_Ltd@compuserve.com